GW00645344

*(above)* Rear Admiral Godfrey, CB
*(left)* Admiral Wilhelm Canaris
*(below)* Ian and·Anne Fleming

# 17F

## The Life of

# IAN FLEMING

## Donald McCormick

Peter Owen · London

PETER OWEN PUBLISHERS
73 Kenway Road London SW5 0RE
Peter Owen books are distributed in the USA by
Dufour Editions Inc. Chester Springs PA 19425–0449

First published in Great Britain 1993
© Donald McCormick 1993

ISBN 0–7206–0888–0

A catalogue record for this book is available from
the British Library

Printed and made in Great Britain

# Acknowledgements

I should like to acknowledge and thank the following for assistance given to me in preparing and writing this book:

The Bodleian Library, Oxford, for permission to quote from the Ian Fleming Collection; Jonathan Cape Ltd and Miss Gaye Poulton for permission to quote from various books by Ian Fleming and from the Fleming–Cape correspondence in Reading University, John Pearson's *Life of Ian Fleming*, *Somerset Maugham* by Ted Morgan and *The James Bond Dossier* by Kingsley Amis; Churchill College, Cambridge, for permission to inspect and quote from their Archives and the Papers of Admiral Godfrey, Patrick Beesley and Donald McLachlan; Collins Harvill and Mr Mark Amory for permission to quote from *The Letters of Anne Fleming*; *The Daily Telegraph* and *The Sunday Telegraph* for permission to quote from various letters and a review; Glidrose Publications and Mr Peter Janson-Smith for help and guidance in a variety of ways; the Goethe Institut of London; the Institut für Zeitgeschichte, Munich; the Lilly Library of Indiana University for permission to quote from its collection of Fleming Papers and books; *The Observer* for permission to quote from an article by Daniel Farson; the Public Record Office, Kew; Reading University and its archivist, Mr Michael Bott, for help in researching the Ian Fleming and Peter Fleming Papers; Reuters News Agency and Mr John G. Entwisle for permission to quote from Reuters' Archives; *The Spectator* for permission to quote from an article by Hugo Vickers; the US Navy Historical Research Center, Washington, DC, and especially to Mr W.J. Morgan, head of its Historical Research Branch; Viking Publishers for permission to quote from Dr David Stafford's *The Silent Game* and *Camp X*.

Also and especially the following individuals: Mr Raymond Benson; Mr Philip Brownrigg; Mr Nicholas Campion; Mr David Chipp of Reuters for permission to quote from an Ian Fleming letter;

Mr Amado Crowley; Miss Amaryllis Fleming and Mr Fergus Fleming for help with photographs; Mr Nicholas Fleming for permission to quote from his father's Papers (the Peter Fleming Papers at Reading University); Mr Charles Fraser-Smith; Mr John Gardner of Charlottesville, Virginia; Sir Alexander Glen for his personal narratives of wartime service; Mrs Kate Grimond, daughter of Mr Peter Fleming; Mr Michael Levien, my editor, for the considerable help and guidance on countless matters which he has given me; Mr Norman Lewis; Mr Ludwik Lubienski of the Polish Combatants' Association, London; the late Mr Michael Mason of Witney; Miss Mona Potterton; Mr Graham Rye, President of the James Bond 007 Fan Club; Dr David Stafford of Toronto; Mr Martin Sterling; Mr Hugo Vickers; Miss Christine Waterman of the Dover Museum; and Dr J. Clive Weeks of Imperial Chemical Industries.

D.McC

# Contents

# Note

The endpapers show (*clockwise from top left*): the Fleming boys when young: (*left to right*) Michael, Richard, Peter and Ian; Rear Admiral Godfrey, Director of Naval Intelligence 1939–42 (*Topical Press*); Admiral Wilhelm Canaris, in charge of German intelligence operations during two world wars (*Hulton Picture Company Ltd*); Ian and Anne Fleming at Jamaica airport two days after their wedding; Christine Granville, wartime British secret agent, found stabbed in a London hotel room, June 1952 (*Popperfoto*); Sir William Stephenson, head of Britain's intelligence network in the USA during the Second World War

# Introduction

I t was in New York during the Second World War that I first met Ian Fleming in the basement bar of the Barbizon-Plaza Hotel. Naval officers awaiting ships still to be built were accommodated at this hotel and spent much of their time in the bar of an evening before venturing further afield.

Fleming was then holding the rank of lieutenant-commander, RNVR, while carrying out the duties of Personal Assistant to the Director of British Naval Intelligence, Admiral Godfrey. He was in the habit of making fairly frequent forays across the Atlantic, thus keeping in touch with the American Office of Naval Intelligence. A tall, handsome and debonair man, with his own effortless yet distinctive power of command, he stood out in any group. I knew hardly anything about his work at that time and even less about the Naval Intelligence Division at the Admiralty. As a mere lieutenant myself, I was somewhat surprised that he should talk to me for more than a few minutes. Then it dawned on me that the sole reason for his doing so was that he wanted to learn something about Combined Operations, the service to which I was attached. This was the service intended to make use of Navy, Army and Air Force personnel in building up an organization which, by means of landing-aircraft, would eventually disembark troops on enemy territory.

Swiftly, Fleming whisked me away to a rather quieter and more discreet bar and proceeded to fire questions at me about life aboard landing-craft. He was – surprisingly, as it seemed to me then – well aware of the stuffiness, and indeed even hostility, of some people inside the Admiralty as well as many senior regular service naval officers on the subject of Combined Operations, but his essentially civilian mind was anxious to know just what made us tick. 'After all,' he commented in a half-laughing, half-lugubrious manner, 'you are supposed to be putting the Army ashore on enemy beaches at some not too distant date.'

At this time prejudice in some sections of the Admiralty against Combined Operations was such that often we were given as crew the poorest quality of Hostilities Only personnel and for leading hands the type who were regarded as either trouble-makers or too difficult to handle in big ships. Thus I think what eventually struck a spark of affinity between Fleming and myself was when he asked me how I dealt with really hopeless cases of Hostilities Only seamen.

'I find the answer is very often to seek out the most useless type and then make him the ship's cook,' I replied.

It was perhaps a rather tactless response and Fleming set down his glass and said: 'Good God! Don't you get a mutiny as a result?'

'Oddly enough, it works,' I said. 'I don't quite know how it works, but it does. I think what happens is that the poor chap is at last content because he is alone and out of sight, tucked away in the ship's galley. There is nobody to get at him. He escapes other chores and is no longer in a position to do any real damage, so gradually he feels happier, more self-confident, and that is reflected in his cooking. Meanwhile his mates will always pop into the galley to give him tips to improve his cooking, or to ensure he doesn't make some appalling gaffe.'

'Hm,' said Fleming, stroking his chin thoughtfully and looking grave. 'Well, let's see how you get along crossing the Atlantic in this flat-bottomed craft with such a cook. I wish you all the luck. But a word of warning – while you chaps are waiting for your craft to be built, you are obviously in mortal danger if you get too talkative in the fleshpots of New York City. There is much to beware of.'

His advice was sound, terse and sophisticated. 'There's a Belgian named Fifi who patronizes the basement bar of the Barbizon-Plaza,' he warned. 'Keep away from her and see your friends do, too. Use force to keep them away if necessary. She's a notorious spy, but we haven't convinced the Americans of this as yet. I am also told that her bedroom conduct is totally reprehensible and unrewarding.'

*Reprehensible and unrewarding!* I shall always remember this example of Fleming's gift for playing with words. He inveighed amusingly on the subject of where and where not to go. 'Yorkville is the German quarter of New York, but it's not really much of a problem unless you go looking for trouble. Much more dangerous is the Spanish quarter of Greenwich Village. That's where you will get your German spies, and their secret weapon is a Mickey Finn. Oh, and by the way, there's a particularly amorous British admiral named A who is known to chase nude girls along the corridors of your current hotel in the middle of the night. Don't get all moral and start putting in reports about him. He may be amorous, but he knows exactly what he is up to and is unlikely to be compromised.' There was a pause and then, still in the most casual of tones, came a warning I was certainly not expecting: 'That redhead you take out drinking – quite a dish, isn't she? Oh, don't look worried. I know exactly what you are going to say – "She's one of us." In a way she is. But she has at least three Vichyites among her current boy-friends and that makes her very suspect indeed. Don't look shocked. She means no deliberate harm, but her other boy-friends might pose a problem for you. You can also be certain that when you are having fun and games with her, the FBI are listening in and having one hell of a peeping Tom's party.'

What impressed me was that Fleming, who seemed to have met me so casually in the Barbizon-Plaza bar, had obviously done his homework on me prior to what appeared to have been an accidental meeting. Obviously he wanted to question a landing-craft commanding officer and had made some inquiries about me (and probably others) in advance of a meeting. The keeping of diaries was strictly forbidden in wartime, though some senior officers seem to have consistently ignored that ruling. As a result I have to rely on memory in re-creating these conversations I had with Fleming. Further conversations I had with him and others in this book are of course not verbatim accounts, but I have recalled the gist of them.

Not long afterwards I left New York to commission my new ship, technically known as an LCI (L), or Landing Craft Infantry (Large). My flotilla was eventually used for ferrying troops and supplies along the North African coast after Operation Torch (the invasion of French territories in North Africa). Algiers was a regular port of call and those of us who liked a little spice and adventure in our night life found it was more free and easy than New York. Some – perhaps most – officers when going ashore confined their activities to drinking on the terrace of the Hotel Aletti. A very few, of whom I was one, took a perverse delight in penetrating the Casbah, or Arab quarter, despite the fact that it was strictly out of bounds to all Allied Services personnel. Perhaps this was in part a reaction to viewing Algiers from the sea first of all. When one approached that city in this way it became a gleaming white monument on a hill, like a grandstand seen from afar, and one longed to absorb its atmosphere. Perhaps also it was exhilarating to flaunt authority and face an element of danger in exploring the narrow cobbled lanes leading up the Casbah Hill in the black-out, knowing full well that some Arabs were quite capable of disembowelling any *roumi* (non-Muslim) they came across.

Lady Diana Cooper, who went with her husband to Algiers in 1943, wrote: 'The Kasbah is a frightening place and we're not allowed in there except under armed escort. It is narrow and terribly smelly, honeycombed with mysterious passage ways.'[1]

The Hampton Court maze is child's play compared with finding one's way around the Casbah. One climbed up a steeply sloping street past the Church of St Croix, once a mosque, the white porch of which used to be the entrance to the Turkish Law Courts of the Aga. On my first night out in Algiers I lost myself in the Casbah. I was with a fellow-officer, Lieutenant Paddy Milton, RNVR, who regarded my exploratory enthusiasm as begging for trouble, when an Algerian girl appeared out of the gloom to come to our rescue. She pointed to her heart and said: 'Je suis Hemo.' Then, telling us to keep close behind her, she led the way up a winding staircase of a narrow lane in which the roofs of houses on either side almost touched those on the other. Up we went, tripping here and there on the rough, cobbled steps, twisting in and out of the tunnelled archways. Once, Hemo pushed us back against a well and motioned us to be still while two burnoused men passed within a yard of where we stood. Eventually she led us to the third floor of a house not far from the top of the Casbah.

She knocked on the door four times quite deliberately. 'Entrez,' called a voice from within.

Inside a garret-like room, lit only by a dim oil lamp, was an enormous bed, canopied at its head by red velvet curtains, draped to make it appear more like a tent than a bed. In this gigantic bed was an equally enormous man feeding grapes to an abnormally large monkey, holding one tattooed arm round it. Speaking in guttural French, he waved the other arm as if in greeting and said: 'Meet Madame Monkey, my beautiful mistress.'

I don't quite know what we had expected Hemo to take us to – probably some form of night-club, as we had asked for somewhere to drink. But we had not bargained on this extraordinary combination of French farce and Poeesque horror. It was the most lasciviously revolting monkey I have ever seen; the man spoke French with a German accent and the only dictionary in the room was a Franco-German one. For good measure the girl, Hemo, wanted me to smuggle her monkey-loving friend Bubu into Spanish Morocco, then nominally neutral, but on the whole unfriendly territory for those of the Allied cause.

I duly reported this story to the proper quarters, but no spies' nest was uncovered, so far as I know. Bubu might have been simply a deserter. Hemo's story was that he was not German but came from Alsace-Lorraine and that he had escaped from Occupied France to Algiers. This much she told us while handing out glasses of wine, for which we paid. Later she produced a bottle of brandy, still hoping I would agree to smuggle Bubu aboard my ship. I explained that it would be strictly against naval orders.

The upshot of this adventure was that I became known as the 'Guide to the Casbah', a title that was more imaginary than factual. On my next visit to Algiers I met a naval officer in a ramshackle hotel in the rue Maréchal Bosquet where we were quietly enjoying a drink in a room by ourselves.

'You know the Casbah rather well, don't you?' I was asked.

'Oh, I wouldn't go as far as that,' I replied cautiously.

'Well, you know your way around it?'

'I must admit I have explored it a little.'

'Don't be so damned coy. What about Bubu and the monkey? What about the gendarme who took you on a conducted tour?

What about *La Sucrerie de l'Amour*? Sweetshop of Love, if you prefer that!'

'Yes, I have met a few Casbah types.'

'You know Marie la Tigre, don't you?'

'I was introduced to her.'

'Then come off the defensive. Let's stop fencing with one another. Look, $17F^2$ wants you to produce an up-to-date map of the Casbah in detail. Every nook, every cranny, every bloody brothel, bar, street, alley, creek and whatnot.'

'But, let's be quite clear on all this: I'm not an expert on the Casbah. I really only know it in the black-out. There must be plenty of maps far more accurate than anything I can draw.'

'There are maps, but they don't tell us enough. Not one is really up to date, and even when it is, there are gaps in the information and not the sort of stuff we want.'

'But surely one of your chaps can do this far better than I? After all, I only come ashore here when my ship's in port and not always then. I don't even speak Arabic.'

'It calls for someone with your nose for trouble and particular eye for the bizarre. Your report on Bubu was thorough and useful. We know perfectly well your limitations in the field of detail. We should never dream of asking you to become involved in technicalities. You will be in port for the next four days. I want the map by the end of that time.'

'But what do I look for?'

There was a silent, cruel grin. 'That's left to your imagination. Places, names and, above all, a list of people to be found in those places. A check, if you like, on what we already know. But you may spot something we have missed. There are, if you must know, far too many German agents still in the Casbah. Maybe their numbers are small, but there are too many of them.'

It did not dawn on me at first that 17F referred to Fleming. Only after I delivered my report and map was this confirmed. But how on earth would Fleming know about my nocturnal trips to the Casbah? Slowly, the answer became clear. My flotilla command-ing officer, Lt-Commander Michael Mason, RNVR, was a friend of Fleming's and had actually been engaged in secret manoeuvres for him in Romania prior to being given command of a landing-craft flotilla. Later he admitted that he had tipped off Fleming in a secret signal, having learned from me that I had met Fleming in New York. 'I thought it might teach you that, whatever you do, the NID learns everything in due course,' he chortled.

The parting shot of the Naval Intelligence man in Algiers was hardly encouraging: 'This will teach you not to go out of bounds in future. Ha! Ha!'

Ha bloody ha! This was not really my *métier* at all. But the next night I set out on another tour of the Casbah, having previously bought myself a guide-book which contained a small and not very detailed map of Algiers itself. It merely showed a maze of lines across the Casbah and no street names. Then, in an obscure second-hand bookshop on the edge of the Casbah, I struck gold. It was entitled *Tout L'Inconnu de la Casbah d'Alger*, by Lucienne Favre, published pre-war in 1933. Though it had no map it contained a wealth of detail from which, bit by bit, I gathered enough information to start on my own cartography.

I must have covered some few miles going backwards and forwards, up and down the convoluted network of cobbled lanes, twisting alleys and rough sandy tracks with such evocative and fascinating names as the rue de Nuit, rue des Oranges, rue de Bain des Lions, rue de la Giraffe, rue des Dattes and the delightfully entitled Hôtel de Lune de Miel.

There was no doubt that the Casbah commanded an ideal view of the whole of Algiers harbour and that any German agent could do a great deal of damage if placed there. In the early months after the North African landings many of the air raids launched on Algiers port were the result of information provided from agents in the Casbah, which escaped damage altogether. Nevertheless I doubt very much that this spying mission of mine helped much towards winning the war. The truth is that a great deal of espionage, especially in wartime, is not only time-wasting and costly, but sometimes pointless. In this case, however, it was at least costless, except to myself.

From North Africa my life switched first to India, then back to the UK for the Normandy landings, and I heard nothing further of or

from Fleming until midsummer 1946. By this time he had left the
Navy and become foreign manager of Kemsley Newspapers in
London. My first job after being demobilized from the Navy was
the editorship of the *Gibraltar Chronicle*, a daily newspaper
catering mainly for British forces personnel stationed on the
Rock. Maybe I had become acclimatized to a life of permanent
adventure with fun both afloat and ashore, but the Gibraltar job
filled me with boredom. Life confined to the garrison of the Rock
was hardly exciting. Indeed, it seemed claustrophobic, with only
occasional visits to Spain to compensate. I begged to be rescued,
and Fleming proved to be my saviour. I wrote to him from
Gibraltar and put up the idea of becoming one of his foreign
correspondents based in the then International Zone of Tangier,
the other side of the Strait of Gibraltar.

I suggested that from such a base I could aim to cover all
north-west Africa from Morocco in the west to Libya in the east
and as far south as French Equatorial Africa, if necessary. My
proposition was a wild gamble, but I stressed that as one could
legally obtain three times the rate of exchange in francs and
pesetas for the pound sterling in Tangier compared with the rate
direct from London, coverage of the whole area would be only a
third of normal costs. Fleming always retained his Scottish zest for
prudence in financial matters and my suggestion paid off. He
made no mention of our previous meeting, or of my Casbah
escapades, but back came a letter which started off: 'I would
be very pleased if you will act as our String Correspondent in
Tangier, with, if possible, tip-off men in Casablanca, Oran, Tunis
and Dakar. . . . I can assure you that we shall be very glad to have
you in the Foreign Service.'[3]

I was delighted. Once again prospects of adventure and excitement loomed large, and so it happened over and over again that
Fleming became the instigator of all manner of surprising missions
for me to undertake, most of them strictly journalistic, but quite a
few of which were sometimes mysterious inquiries for Fleming
himself. For the next fourteen years I was in the closest touch with
this Richard Hannay of a newspaper executive, and a few years
later I returned to London to be in an office adjoining his own.

Fleming has been portrayed as a playboy who liked to fantasize and a snob who kept his staff at a distance. This is not a true portrayal. He was unique in the way in which he cared for and looked after his staff, especially those overseas. He made it his job to know all about his correspondents, their families and their problems.

Later he recalled to me my mission in the Casbah. He said: 'André Gide has written that Algiers is "the wickedest city in the world". Why don't you write a book called *The Wicked City*? You could bring in all about the Sweetshop of Love and that character who ran it, Marie la Tigre of Toulouse.'

After further prompting from Fleming that was just what I did, though he asked me to keep his name out of the book. Some years later when I had acquired the address of The Oast House, Liptraps Lane, High Brooms, just outside Tunbridge Wells, he commented: 'That sounds an erotic piece of witchery. You've done *The Wicked City*, why don't you now do *The Wicked Village*, making your Oast House the central theme?'

'Bearing in mind the laws of libel, it would have to be an imaginary village,' I replied.

'Make it just that. Simply transport yourself and your family and your oast-house home into some imaginary village. You should be able to dig up some exciting rural gossip and skulduggery to fit the title. Keep Liptraps Lane, if you can. I really like that splendidly named thoroughfare.'

Again I followed his advice.

Fleming always tried to make the task of working for him fun. It seems only fair that I should try to repay his considerations by making some tribute to him. At the same time I shall attempt to dispel some of the superficial, snide and often purely fanciful comments about him which have been both said and written, often by those envious of his swift success after *Casino Royale* was published.

'The Chocolate Sailor' was what the late Lord Beaverbrook called Ian Fleming, borrowing a phrase that had been conjured up by some of Fleming's jealous colleagues at the Admiralty. They not only envied his popularity with women, but the manner in which he handled his senior officers as though they were equals and not in the deferential manner to which they were accustomed. The late William Plomer, who served with Fleming in the Naval

Intelligence Division, described Fleming as

> . . . decidedly a man of our time, but in any age such an
> uncommon personality, such varied gifts and high spirits, would
> make a strong impression. He made one feel one had to try and
> live up to his own standard of alertness, to keep tuned up, and
> to move at his own quick tempo. He seemed always to take the
> shortest distance between two points in the shortest possible
> time, and although he didn't suffer bores gladly, his appetite for
> life, his curiosity and quick understanding, and his admiration of
> what was well done used generally to bring out the best in other
> people. . . . His head was never turned by his enormous
> popular success. But popular success often rankles with the
> unsuccessful, and in the natural course of things he was exposed
> to envy; this was sometimes to be seen in print, but I never
> heard him take any notice of it.[4]

This carefully considered appraisal of Fleming helps to put the
record straight and to give a more balanced picture of a remarkable character. Yet even in recent times Fleming has been portrayed – especially by some who never knew him – as being Bond
and nothing but Bond. It is true that he put a lot of himself into
the character of Bond, but in reality he was much more like the
character 'M' than Bond. In fact he would have made an admirable head of the British Secret Service, as he was a first-class
administrator, a sound judge of character and the kind of man for
whom an agent in the field would love to work.

When Charles Dance was chosen to play the role of Fleming in
the ITV film *Goldeneye*, in 1989, he was asked to read everything
Fleming had written and also all that had been written about him.
The result was, we are told, that 'having done his homework,
Dance concluded that Fleming was a melancholic who used sex,
tobacco and alcohol to insulate himself from his own disenchanted
view of the world'.[5] This is a distorted view of the real Fleming.
Yet again and again in recent years he has been presented as a
mere playboy who rarely took life seriously. It is true that he was
easily bored and that his show of boredom may have been taken
for melancholia. But for anyone who held the kind of posts
Fleming filled, it would be essential to be dismissive of things that

were of no consequence: to this extent boredom was a defensive weapon against getting involved in unnecessary details.

It is partly because of the need for a reappraisal of the whole Fleming life story that I have written this biography. The first biography, by John Pearson, was a detailed and lengthy work with much documentation,[6] but it was not then possible to tell everything about Fleming, for a variety of reasons.

There is a great deal that can still be learned from a careful study of Fleming's books, yet envious critics have often ventured into attacking his writing without ever having read any of them. The late Malcolm Muggeridge wrote an article in the American periodical *Esquire* only a few months after Fleming's death. Muggeridge repeated this article with certain changes in the London *Observer* in June 1965, saying he had read only one of Fleming's books and had no intention of reading any more, calling him 'a Peter Pan of the bordellos' and a man with 'squalid aspirations'. At the same time Muggeridge claimed that he knew Ian well, was a great friend of his wife's and frequently enjoyed their hospitality. Ian's brother, Peter, was prompted to write to *The Observer* saying: 'To vilify publicly, within a few months of his death, a friend from whom he had received nothing but kindness is not the sort of thing that it would occur to many of us to do.'[7]

Fleming was a restless man, not satisfied with just one talent but always seeking new talents in himself. He was the kind of person who really needed two jobs, or at least a full-time job and an important hobby. This was yet another of his ploys for defeating his real enemy – boredom. He was always happiest when he was building ideas, an adult setting up one idea on top of another rather as a child builds with toy bricks. He had a deeply rooted ethical sense which he certainly never flaunted. He abhorred long, intense discussions whether on business or emotional matters, preferring to round things off quickly with a quip or sardonic joke. He also preferred people to respond in exactly the same way.

There is much about Fleming that has not yet been told, some of it breathtakingly surprising and giving a different picture of the man. But then he had a capacity for springing surprises.

# 1

## The Ghost of a Dead Father

Please, God, make me like father.[1]

I an Fleming was a few days short of his ninth birthday when his
father, Major Valentine Fleming, was killed in action in the
First World War. This was a most untimely age at which to lose a
parent, especially one who had always been portrayed to him as a
hero and someone whose example he must always follow.

The legend of Valentine Fleming was built up in the early years
of Fleming's life, not only by a tribute to his father by Winston
Churchill, but by the posthumous award of a DSO and, finally,
and perhaps most importantly, by a mother who constantly in-
stilled into Fleming that he must grow up to be like his father. It
has been said that Valentine Fleming was very fond of his second
son, Ian, whom he called 'Johnny'. On the other hand Fleming
himself in later life insisted that he could not recall much about his
father. The probability is that he had been fed so much with other
people's memories of his father that they obscured his own and he
began to feel he never knew him.

Yet it is true that for many years Ian Fleming lived in the
shadow of his dead father. Mrs Fleming, who took upon herself
the role of stern father as well as kindly mother, constantly urged
him to remember his dead parent even to the extent of encouraging him to end his nightly prayers as a child with the words quoted
at the beginning of this chapter. Who can say for sure what
psychological effect this had on a boy not yet in his teens? It may
well explain how Ian came to be almost, though not quite, the odd
man out among the family Valentine Fleming produced. By the
time he was in his teens Ian was the exception among all the

Fleming boys in rejecting the family's traditional love of such pursuits as hunting, shooting and fishing. He liked neither horses nor dogs.

There were two distinct cultures in the Fleming family. On his father's side there was the background of a family who had come up the hard way from relative poverty in Dundee two generations ago, making a virtue of Calvinistic values and proud of being Scots. Grandfather Robert Fleming, one of seven children, a member of the Free Church of Scotland, was so successful in his financial ventures that, in 1873, at the age of twenty-eight, he helped form the Scottish-American Investment Trust. He soon became a millionaire, sending his two sons to Eton to be educated. In 1906, Valentine Fleming, newly elected Member of Parliament for South Oxfordshire, married Evelyn Beatrice Ste Croix Rose. Her family background was quite different to Valentine's – almost cosmopolitan – and claimed English, Irish, Scots and Huguenot ancestry. Just as Valentine Fleming was dutiful, conventional and cautious, Evelyn was conscientious, but occasionally unconventional and erratic.

It was Grandfather Robert who really created what became an important and talented Fleming dynasty, and some of the family went out to Canada and New Zealand and established roots there. Originally, all the Flemings had been Gaelic speaking, but even among the poorest members of the family the emphasis was on providing a sound education for their children regardless of the cost. In 1929 Robert Fleming, mindful of his father's poverty in his early years, gave £155,000 to the city of Dundee for the purpose of clearing up the slums and providing better housing. He also helped many poor relations, including some aunts in Kansas City.

How all this affected Ian Fleming it is not easy to assess. Certainly he was acutely conscious of the problems which lack of money could bring – sympathetically so, as he was always concerned about sheltering his friends and his staff from such problems. Though he often gambled at bridge and casinos (sometimes to get background material for his books), he frequently denounced gambling, saying 'it goes against my Quaker origins'. No doubt he was joking when he used the word 'Quaker', because I am assured by members of the Fleming family of today that they have no Quaker origins.

Robert Fleming and his wife showed the same sense of being part of the community when they settled at Nettlebed in Oxfordshire as when they had lived in Dundee. In 1919, as part of the Peace Day celebrations after the First World War, they gave a tea in the village hall to all children under the age of fifteen, each child receiving souvenir beakers. Some idea of how this family looked upon what they regarded as their duties to the community may be seen in what Winston Churchill said about Valentine Fleming after his death. He described him as 'one of those younger Conservatives who easily and liberally combine loyalty to party ties with a broad, liberal outlook upon affairs and a total absence of class prejudice. He was most earnest and sincere in his desire to make things better for the great body of the people'.[2] Churchill was at that time a member of the Liberal Party, while Valentine Fleming was Conservative MP for South Oxfordshire.

One of Eve Fleming's many claims about her widely diversified ancestry was that John of Gaunt was one of her forbears. Born in Ghent and married to Blanche, heiress of the Duchy of Lancaster, he was created Duke of Lancaster, the name Eve Fleming insisted should be added to that of Ian when the latter was born on 28 May 1908, in London. 'Remember you are a Lancaster' was yet another of her reminders to Ian of what she called 'the importance of ancestry'.[3]

There is no doubt that Eve was a devoted mother to all her sons: Peter, the eldest, Ian, Michael and Richard. She gave a great deal more time to them than did most mothers of her class in those days. This, however, was to some extent spoiled by the way she 'played father' as well. Nevertheless, though the latter tactics sometimes embarrassed her sons, she was a versatile woman who mixed Bohemian informality with periods of strict formality. Among her many talents were those she applied to cooking, carpentry, sewing, gardening and playing the violin. It is perhaps not altogether without relevance that Ian called his mother 'M', the same initial that he later gave to James Bond's chief.

It has been suggested that Ian was jealous of the prowess of his elder brother and that they could not stand each other's company.

'Nothing was further from the truth,' declares Peter Fleming's biographer, Duff Hart-Davis. 'As a boy Peter stood in physical awe of his younger and much larger brother – so much so that when he came into his presence he would tremble with apprehension. . . . Their friendship remained strong even though they seldom met.'[4]

One reason, of course, why they did not meet frequently in later life was that Ian disliked the field sports that were indulged in at the ancestral home at Merrimoles in Oxfordshire, which Peter eventually took over.

During the First World War, while her husband was away on Army service, Eve Fleming chose a preparatory school for her two elder sons, this being the somewhat unconventional establishment of Durnford in Dorsetshire. The aim of the headmaster was to give the boys greater freedom in the belief that it would make them happier. In fact the result was a lack of discipline and an increase in bullying. It was not perhaps the best preparation for Eton.

Ivar Bryce, almost a lifelong friend of Ian's, recalls meeting the Fleming boys at the age of eight in 1914 and playing with them on the beach at Bude, building sand-castles. Later Bryce and the Flemings were at Eton together. In an admiring tribute to Ian Bryce writes of him: 'While not desperately competitive he would try violently to run the fastest and furthest, to jump the longest and highest, to climb the steepest . . . and in every way expend the last drop of a furious energy on any achievement that presented itself'.[5]

Bryce and Ian had a Scottish ancestry in common. Bryce's paternal great-grandfather was a Scot who had set out to make his fortune in Peru. His father had fought in the Boer War with the Coldstream Guards. This friendship of Bryce and Fleming ran on parallel lines: after they left Eton as young bachelors they pursued girls together. In the Second World War, while Ian was in Naval Intelligence, Bryce was doing espionage work in South and Central America on behalf of the Allies.

Eve Fleming kept on the family's country home, the mock-Gothic mansion of Merrimoles, but Ian felt much happier when he was either away at school or on occasional visits to London when his mother visited there. The several hundred acres of rough shooting land and stables held no attraction for him. He was much delighted when, in 1923, his mother moved to Chelsea Embankment in London, and turned three houses into one. She called it Turner's House after the painter, Joseph Turner, who is said to have lived in one of the three original houses.

Fleming went to Eton in 1921 and his housemaster was E.V. Slater, who placed great stress on rigid discipline and all-round efficiency. It was a house with an atmosphere that could hardly be called relaxed. Fleming has described James Bond's career at Eton as 'brief and undistinguished'. This, it has been suggested, was an autobiographical touch but, if so, Fleming was being too modest. He may not have distinguished himself academically or in conventional team games such as cricket, but, as Bryce has suggested, he was an outstanding athlete. While his brother Peter became Captain of the Oppidans, Ian was highly successful in such sports as running and jumping. In 1924 he won seven out of ten events in the Eton Junior Sports, a feat not achieved either previously or since, and in the Senior Sports later he was Victor Ludorum for two years in succession. This later achievement has only once been equalled. In 1926 he won the hurdles at Stamford Bridge in the Public Schools' Athletics Contest.

There is some evidence that Fleming and his housemaster did not have an easy relationship and that Ian was just as likely to be disobedient at school as he occasionally was at home. He was not the type to be interested in what he regarded as 'academic irrelevances', his very own phrase, and his reading as a boy was much more likely to be Buchan, Edgar Allan Poe, Robert Louis Stevenson and Edgar Wallace than Thackeray, Dickens and Trollope. He also took a romantic interest in Scotland and Scottish history, while his passion for finding buried treasure both as a boy and later as an adult sprang out of the kind of literature he enjoyed.

Despite the fact that he achieved no outstanding scholastic triumphs at Eton, Fleming took a great interest in literature and, realist that he was, especially in literature that had an impact on life. William Plomer has recorded that Ian while at Eton 'pounced appreciatively at that time upon the first book of a then unknown writer – a book which in its season was probably an outstanding worst seller, but which turned out to have a lasting influence. This was nothing like a half-baked schoolboy of the flannelled-fool variety, but already a young man with a mind searching for facts, pressing forward to discover what the world was like'.[6] This was a reference to Plomer's first novel, a work called *Turbott Wolfe* which was published in 1926, while Fleming was still at school. 'He got hold of it, read it and was excited by it,' writes Plomer. 'He had almost certainly never heard of me before, and I can't remember what put him on to the book. He might have been guided by his sharp flair, like that of a mine-detector, for a new threat to dullness and complacency.'[7]

At any rate Fleming wrote to Plomer about the book, which seems to have made a lasting impression on him. Some critics found *Turbott Wolfe* disturbing: this was indeed the author's intention, for he recognized and asserted that life includes the head-on collision of violent forces. It was a few years later that Fleming actually met Plomer, inviting him to a party in Chelsea given by his mother. 'At that first encounter he struck me as no mere conventional young English man-of-the-world of his generation. He showed more character, a much quicker brain and a promise of something dashing or daring. Like a mettlesome young horse, he seemed to show the whites of his eyes and to smell some battle from afar.'[8]

It is said by some who knew him that about this time Fleming started writing poetry and that ultimately he put together a collection of verse, which he entitled *The Black Daffodil*. He is alleged to have burnt all copies of it. Another piece of his writing, also said to have been destroyed, was a short story, which he called 'The True Tale of Captain Kidd's Treasure', a theme that interested him throughout his life.

There is no indication that Ian wrote anything for *The Eton College Chronicle*. However, judging from the contents of that journal, this is not altogether surprising. Ian's nephew, Fergus Fleming, another Old Etonian, told me that he found the contents of the *Chronicle* in the early twenties 'very dry and proper and offering only minimal opportunity for an aspiring writer. From my experience of Eton, schoolboy society is roughly divided into the "hearties" and the "swots". The division, I imagine, would have been even more pronounced in those days. I don't think Ian, at that age, had the capacity or inclination to be other than a "hearty"'.

There was one occasion while Fleming was at Eton in 1924 when he made an out-of-bounds trip to the British Empire Exhibition at Wembley on a motor bike. He was spotted, reprimanded, but let off any punishment. There were also a few escapades with girls outside of school, even though such contacts were strictly forbidden. His other great interest at the time was in cars, a subject that occupied a prominent place in the conversation of public schoolboys of the period.

That he was still devoted to the memory of his father is clearly shown by the fact that even at that age he had framed a newspaper clipping of Churchill's tribute to him and kept it wherever he was. The nightly instruction of his mother had had an effect. It would seem that he kept this framed reminder all his life, and Lt Alan N. Schneider, of the US Navy, who was his close colleague in the Second World War, recalls that it was 'hung in his [Ian's] room at the Carlton Hotel where he was staying when I knew him'.[9]

In his last year at Eton Ian Fleming was unable to compete in some of the sporting events because of an accident in which he broke his nose while playing football, necessitating an operation. If anything, this broken nose gave his looks a touch of panache and made him more attractive to women. Alan Schneider, whose own nose was broken while boxing, said that he and Ian used to compare noses: 'I thought this made him look like a handsome pirate.'[10]

It became apparent that Ian would not make it to Oxford, though he himself was not enthusiastic about going to university. His mother was very disappointed about this and suggested he should try for Sandhurst, with a view to an Army career. David Herbert, who was at Eton at the same time as Fleming, says that though they were in different houses, 'strangely enough we were both sent to the same "crammer" after leaving Eton. It was run by a Major Trevor. We can neither of us have been particularly bright, or we would not have been sent to such a place by our respective parents!' A friendship was formed between the two Old Etonians and this proved invaluable when war came, as will be shown in due course.

After a certain amount of special coaching for the Royal Military College examination Fleming passed with flying colours. He was sixth in an entrance examination for the whole country, which suggests that he must have worked quite hard at the crammer course. But Officer Cadet Fleming soon became convinced that Army life was not for him and he thoroughly disliked the whole training system at Sandhurst. This is neither surprising nor unusual: there were many who quite enjoyed life in the Services in wartime but who knew instinctively that they would hate it in peacetime. So Fleming, determined to take matters into his own hands, wrote a postcard to the Commandant of the Royal Military College, indicating that he wished to leave.

Undeterred by these two apparent failures, Eve Fleming decided that the Foreign Office might provide a suitable career for Ian, and with this in mind she gave him a modest allowance. To prepare him for the Foreign Office examinations she decided to send him to a small school, the Tennerhof, run by Ernan Forbes Dennis and his wife at Kitzbühel in the Tyrol. Mrs Fleming had made the most careful inquiries about this school, especially among parents whose children had received education there, and her decision to send both Peter and Ian to this establishment proved to be a wise one. Not only did Ian learn to speak French and German fluently, but he learned some Russian while he was there.

Forbes Dennis, who had been badly wounded in the First World War, had been Intelligence Officer at Marseilles towards the end of hostilities and after the Armistice was Passport Control Officer in Vienna. In 1917 he had married Phyllis Bottome, the daughter of the Revd William Macdonald Bottome of New York. Her first book, *Raw Material*, was published in 1905, but it was not until after the war that she came into her own as a writer. For most of her life she moved in what are sometimes tactfully called Intelligence circles and it is probable that to some extent she was involved in such work. She wrote one spy novel, *The Life-Line* (1946). There is no doubt that she encouraged Ian to write; indeed, under her mentorship he wrote an unpublished short story, 'Death on Two Occasions'. 'If a writer is true to his characters, they will give him his plot' was her advice.

There has been much talk that at about this time Fleming was considered to be in disgrace with family and friends. This is a gross exaggeration. It is no easy task to know exactly what to do after leaving school, and to find the right niche in life may take years rather than months. This was the case with Ian Fleming. Another fallacy is the story that at the Forbes Dennises' school he was always the odd boy out, the one who never settled down properly. Peter Fleming had been sent to the same school before Ian and he hated it.

Again it has been suggested that Fleming disgraced himself and his family by failing to be accepted in the Foreign Service. Here again the facts hardly bear this out: he finished seventh in a year when some sixty-two candidates were competing for only five vacancies. He may have felt somewhat of a failure because he had not settled into a career, but his real concern was that he was still dependent on an allowance from his mother. Nevertheless he still hadn't made up his mind what he wanted to do in life and he angered his grandfather by refusing to go into the family banking firm after he failed to enter the Foreign Service. At one time his worried mother considered sending him to Australia, though quite what she had in mind for him there is not clear.

During his time at Kitzbühel Fleming went to Munich to perfect his German by staying with a local family, enlisting as an external student at the university. Later he went to Geneva to improve his French. He gave every indication of enjoying himself, despite the fact that he suffered from periods of 'black melancholy' while at the Tennerhof School.

The word melancholia tends to give the impression of some kind of deep depression. In fact it was a word that Fleming himself used to describe some of his moods, but this again was Ian speaking with tongue slightly in cheek. When he spoke of melancholia, no doubt he meant boredom: he was very easily bored. He loathed small talk, and avoided the kinds of parties where it was the norm. He was not a snob, but he kept people he thought boring at a distance, and when he did so as a young man it was often misconstrued as arrogance or melancholia.

The Forbes Dennises seem to have overreacted to reports of Fleming's so-called melancholia. They decided that Fleming was a case for a psychiatrist. Maybe they had been influenced by a worried mother. In any event, Forbes Dennis eventually persuaded Fleming to see the celebrated Austrian psychologist Alfred Adler, for whom both Forbes Dennis and his wife had the greatest admiration. As this couple were themselves Adlerians in their approach to teaching, it was probably their version of the Adlerian philosophy that had the greatest impact. In later life Fleming was the first to play down pessimism and to encourage optimism even when the outlook was bleakest.

An astonishing comment on these aspects of Fleming's character was made by a Harley Street psychiatrist, Dr Joshua Bierer, when giving evidence in a London court in defence of the wrestler Fred Rondel, one-time strong-arm man for the property racketeer Peter Rachman. Dr Bierer compared Rondel, who was convicted of running an unlicensed gaming house, to Fleming, alleging that 'Ian Fleming was like a common animal'. Later in his consulting-rooms Dr Bierer elaborated on this theme, saying:

> Fleming's mother had sent him to Austria to see the great psychiatrist, Dr Alfred Adler, because she was in despair. Her son was dissipating his life away in London, drinking and whoring. At that time I was a student of Dr Adler. One Sunday I was asked to go urgently to the ski resort of Kitzbühel to treat Fleming.
>
> Each night he was out with a different girl, and he must have slept with most of the girls in town in a short while. He was a totally ruthless young man. He didn't consider anyone. Like all psychopaths, he couldn't tell right from wrong. You could say he had the bad bits of James Bond in his character. I believe the world of fantasy Fleming wrote about was his salvation.[11]

In effect what Dr Bierer was saying was that James Bond saved Fleming from landing in a mental hospital. In my view, this is not only an exaggerated and erroneous conception of Fleming's problems at that time, but an unpleasant slur on his character. I am citing Dr Bierer because his assertion requires a positive refutation. The language used suggests that Bierer rather than Fleming was the psychopath. His talk about James Bond is ridiculous, as Bond was not even created by Fleming until more than twenty years later. If Bierer really did confer with Fleming, one wonders what kind of an effect his theorizing might have had on a young man. My own deduction is that Ian Fleming learned early on in life not only how easy it is for a human being to be misunderstood by others, but that it is vital in dealing with other humans to let them know that you understand them and their problems. This was the attitude he forcefully and effectively adopted in dealing with people both in the Navy in the Second World War and with his huge team of foreign correspondents afterwards. It would have been hard to find any other employer to compare to him in this respect. In other words he very quickly learned the lessons of how he himself was misunderstood.

Bierer was appointed to the Teaching Institute in Individual Psychology in Berlin in 1928, but with the rise of Nazism he came to England and, after serving in the RAMC in the war, founded the social psychotherapy centre which in 1946 was named the Marlborough Day Hospital.

Ian enjoyed himself at Kitzbühel, just as he did in Munich and Geneva, and he must have had a number of amatory affairs, though not in the style of Dr Bierer's hyped-up version of his activities. The use of the word 'hype' is not unreasonable here: Dr Bierer actually told the London *Times* that 'Ian Fleming had the type of personality which, if he had not found a role in which to excel, would have led to the gutter, a mental hospital or prison.'[12]

It was not, of course, until long after Fleming's death that Bierer made these comments, otherwise there would have been a case for the victim of his abuse to bring a libel action. It is true that Fleming made many women friends, not only while he was at Kitzbühel, but later in Geneva and Munich. With some of these he kept in touch for a long time. To one such, Lisi Popper, with whom he went skiing, he left £500 in his will. At one time it seemed as if he might become engaged to the daughter of a Swiss landowner, but two factors prevented a development of this relationship. First, his mother was quick to point out (as parents did in those days) that financially he could not yet afford to keep a wife and, secondly, there was another German girl to whom he was

increasingly attracted. This was Vanessa Hoffmann, of whom
more will be heard later: it was she who interested Fleming in the
arts of astrology and some other occult sciences.

What appealed to Fleming about girls on the Continent was
how much they differed from the British girls he had so far
encountered. He found the continental girls more fun, more sophisticated and better educated. He confided to Alan Schneider that
he had 'never really cared too much about the English girls – he
said they didn't bathe enough and they didn't know the first thing
about making love'. He was popular with the girls on the Continent and as a result received all manner of social invitations. His
friend Ivar Bryce has summed up the amatory aspects of Fleming's life and philosophy on love:

> He had such magnetism and generosity of heart that to know
> him well was to be filled with affection for him. . . . There had
> been a series of these appealing nymphs throughout his life. The
> lady's side followed a similar pattern composed of glamorous
> flirtation, abject slavery and fond nostalgia, in that order. They
> always remained friends, and kindness and help of all
> descriptions could be relied on from Ian whenever required.[13]

It should, however, be stressed that this was only the rec-
reational side of Fleming's life at the time. He was working hard
during this period and, what was more, studying a variety of
subjects. He had enrolled as an external student at the Univer-
sities of Geneva and Munich, and in his Foreign Office examination, far from being a total failure, he obtained 70 per cent in both
French and German and 56 per cent for his Russian. During this
period he read widely, especially in German and Russian, and
obtained a Swiss *certificat* in anthropology.

Gradually, he came to see his future as a writer. Common sense
suggested that a salaried job was the safest and his mother agreed.
As always, she set about trying to find him a worthwhile job while
he was still weighing the pros and cons. She approached Sir
Roderick Jones, the head of Reuters, who agreed to consider an
application from her son. When he wrote to Sir Roderick, Fleming gave as references Lord d'Abernon, Forbes Dennis and

Brigadier-General Robert White, mentioning that he had 'a good knowledge of psychology' and that for a short period he had worked for the Austrian Government in the Secretariat of the League of Nations in the Section for Intellectual Cooperation.

In October 1931 Fleming was given a six months' trial with Reuters at a starting salary of £150 a year. To a young man with big ideas and extravagant tastes this would have seemed modest indeed, and perhaps it explains why in later life he often said that he had known poverty. However, he must have been much appreciated by the powers-that-be at Reuters because his salary was soon increased to £206.5s. a year and, by the time he left Reuters, he was receiving £300 a year.

In an early report on Fleming his news editor, Bernard Rickatson-Hatt, stated that 'so far he has made an excellent impression. His languages are sound and his manners agreeable. He suffers perhaps from a slight F.O. [Foreign Office] bump'. A little later another of the news editors' memoranda read: '. . . he is accurate, painstaking and methodical. He also has a good business instinct'.[14]

During the two years Fleming was with Reuters he had all-round experience. Some of the time he worked as a sub-editor, and he was also given the task of working on obituaries. It is recorded that he brought no fewer than five hundred obituaries up to date. His reporting assignments ranged from coverage of the Coupe des Alpes motor rally and the International Alpine Trials to assignments in Berlin and Moscow. His most outstanding assignment was undoubtedly his coverage of the show trial in Moscow of a group of British engineers. This brought Reuters world-wide praise.

The British engineers had gone to the Soviet Union to work on various construction projects: they were charged with sabotage and espionage so that they could be used as scapegoats for short-comings in Stalin's plans for the industrialization of the USSR. Reuters had a correspondent in Moscow, Robin Kinkead, but Rickatson-Hatt decided that he needed help in the coverage of a trial of such international interest. Fleming was the man he chose, probably on the strength of his knowledge of Russian. 'Absolutely everything depends upon our getting the story out first' he was told.

Fleming accepted the challenge with alacrity and, on arriving in Moscow, immediately investigated the facts behind this strange trial, the layout of the court and how best to get his copy dispatched speedily. On 12 April 1933 he sent the following pre-trial dispatch:

> As the famous clock in the Kremlin Tower strikes twelve the six
> Metropolitan-Vickers English employees will enter a room
> which has been daubed with blue in the Trades Union Hall and
> thronged with silent multitudes in order to hear an impassive
> Russian voice read for four or five hours the massive indictment
> which may mean death or exile. Within the packed room there
> will be a feeling of the implacable working of the soulless
> machinery of Soviet justice calling to account six Englishmen to
> decide whether the Metropolitan-Vickers raid was a vast bungle
> or a Machiavellian coup.

At one stroke Fleming put the whole trial in perspective. He soon received congratulatory cables from London, informing him that his stories were surpassing those of his competitors. By such forthright reporting as the item just quoted he was also putting himself at risk of being arrested. At the same time the strain of covering the trial was considerable. He was filing on average two thousand words a day during the trial and he had to make advance arrangements for reporting on the verdicts. He had a boy waiting outside a window where the trial was taking place to catch his verdict message in the sheet below.

In the end the sentences were more lenient than expected. Two of the engineers were given prison sentences of three and two years respectively, while three others were ordered to be deported. Fleming's speedy reporting was praised by his fellow-journalists in a cable they sent Sir Roderick Jones, in which they affirmed their 'high opinion of his journalistic ability. He has given us all a run for our money'.[15]

For good measure Fleming had even tried to get an interview with Stalin while he was in Moscow. He was not successful, but he managed to obtain a signed letter of refusal. Duff Hart-Davis in his biography of Peter Fleming states that when Ian's brother left for a trip to Russia he took with him 'a signed letter from Stalin which his brother Ian had acquired a year before in Moscow while covering the Metro-Vickers trial. He showed it on a number of occasions to use as a kind of super-visa to bluff his way out of awkward situations'.


When Fleming returned to London he was lauded on all sides, even being asked to give a report on his experiences to the Foreign Office. He had had what he afterwards described as 'the most momentous year in my life to date not forgetting my court case'. This was a reference to his having been fined three guineas with costs at Oxford for driving an unlicensed car. He did not appear at the court, saying he was attending the World Economic Conference, which the magistrate commented was 'a somewhat extraordinary excuse'.

Fleming was concerned about his low salary even though it was supplemented by a modest allowance from his mother. As a reward for his work in Moscow Sir Roderick Jones offered him the post of assistant general manager of Reuters in the Far East at a salary of £800 per annum. In many ways this post attracted him, but it so happened that another, totally different appointment was also being offered him, this time in a City stockbroker's office. The Reuters job would have given him an office to himself in Shanghai, then an exciting place to be in. He later confirmed to Rickatson-Hatt that his mother was primarily responsible for persuading him to accept the offer in the City.

It was in December 1933 that Fleming left Reuters to join the firm of Cull and Company. His financial affairs, along with those of his mother and brothers, had been severely affected by the unexpected news that his grandfather, who had recently died, had made no provision for them but had left his considerable fortune to his widow for her lifetime and after that to his second son, Philip. Ian felt this was grossly unfair, though it may well have been an oversight in old age by his grandfather.

The job with Cull and Company did not last long. In June 1935 Fleming became a partner in the well-established stockbroking firm of Rowe and Pitman.

# 2

## *From the City to the NID*

Of the staff in Room 39 . . . Ian Fleming was the most vivid
and became the best-known personality. . . . He was a skilled
fixer and vigorous showman.[1]

I t has been suggested that Fleming's mother tried too hard
early on to dictate to her son and plan his career for him. This
is unfair. Strong-minded she may have been, but it should be
remembered that to some extent she had to play a father's role as
well. All the evidence suggests that she, and she alone, saved him
from the many mistakes which enterprising young men were apt
to make in those days. In persuading Fleming to leave Reuters
and take up a job in the City, which ultimately gained him a
partnership, she realized that he needed to think in terms of
money as well as pure enjoyment. With this in view, he had made
up his mind while at Reuters to take book collecting seriously and
to build up a useful and valuable collection of his own.

It was the German girl, Vanessa Hoffmann, whom he met in
Munich, who first interested Fleming in book collecting. It was
her idea that he should collect what she called 'books about ideas
and exciting new theories', pointing him in the direction of Steiner,
Jung and Freud as well as Binet, the creator of IQ. Vanessa, who
was playing in an orchestra in Munich at the time Fleming met
her, had been educated in Zurich and Vienna. She was also a keen
student of astrology and had interested Ian in the subject. Once,
when he was asked how he came to start this collection, Fleming
told the late Cyril Connolly that 'probably Forbes Dennis and
Phyllis gave me the idea and certainly Percy Muir gave me every
encouragement. But the real inspiration came from a German girl

I met in Munich. She said that even if I got fed up with collecting them, I could always be sure of selling them for far more than I originally paid'.[2]

As noted, Fleming built up his book collection partly under the guidance of Percy Muir, who at that time was an antiquarian bookseller, being a director of Elkin Mathews of Grosvenor Street, London. Much later Muir became President of the Antiquarian Booksellers' Association and Fleming himself became founder and proprietor of *The Book Collector*, the British antiquarian quarterly. In the mid-1930s Fleming had set himself up in a house in Cheyne Walk, Chelsea, and, when he joined Rowe and Pitman, he felt able to splash out rather more extravagantly on building up his collection of books. A bill from Elkin Mathews for books purchased, dated 18 June 1935, shows that he had spent some £62.4s.1d. on some thirty-three books, including no fewer than eight of Einstein's works. Not a large sum by modern standards, but quite considerable in the thirties.

This was undoubtedly a period of experimentation for Fleming, during which he tried to find the right career for himself, while he remained anxious to increase his knowledge of a wide range of subjects, and intent upon building a wide range of contacts. His book collecting was closely linked to his various interests, Fleming describing his collection as 'first editions of all original thoughts since 1748'. The work referring to 1748 was Leonhard Euler's book, *Analytical Mathematics*, published in Lausanne in that year – hardly a subject, one might assume, that would have held any appeal for him. This collection of more than a thousand books has now been acquired by the Lilly Library of Indiana University and is described as 'the Ian Fleming Collection of 19th–20th Century Source Material concerning Western Civilization'. Percy Muir has given a detailed account of how it was accumulated. Though the idea was Fleming's, much of the work involved was Muir's, and Muir stressed that the collection was made in a remarkably short time, largely concentrated in the latter half of the 1930s.[3]

'Modern civilization was fashioned in the nineteenth century,' declared Percy Muir in a précis he wrote for the Lilly Library Collection of Fleming's books. He went on:

It is hardly an exaggeration to say that the world of 1800 was much closer in its essentials to prehistoric Egypt than to the world of 1970. . . . The Fleming Collection was an attempt to gather together, in first editions, the original contributions of the scientists and practical workers, the total body of whose work has been responsible for the modern revolution. . . . Near the end of Fleming's collecting, an attempt to represent the important literary figures of the period was begun. Although it did not progress very far, this section includes first editions of Goethe, Byron, Balzac, Butler, Dickens, Maeterlinck, Maupassant, Lautréamont, Pater, Kipling, Proust, Rilke, Schiller, Schnitzler, Scott, Gertrude Stein, Turgenev, Zola. . . .[4]

Fleming insisted that he was passionately interested in all genuinely new ideas and inventions – books which, he said, 'started something', or 'made things happen'. The range of his collection was catholic and covered many new philosophies and inventions. The invention of the electric battery and Freud's *The Interpretation of Dreams* lay alongside the *Essai sur l'inégalité des races humaines* of Hitler's mentor, the Comte de Gobineau, and *Darkest England* by William Booth, the founder of the Salvation Army. Subjects covered included Einstein's theories of relativity, Lenin's earliest works, criminology and fingerprints, the splitting of the atom, the first photographs of the so-called canals of Mars, the rules of table tennis, the origins of auction bridge and *The Doctrine of Chances: Or a Method of Calculating the Probability of Events in Play*. The latter was probably the oldest book in the whole collection and one obtained after he had styled his huge pile as dating from 1748.

While Fleming was inspired by his interest in many different subjects, no doubt his canny Scottish background encouraged him to look upon the collection as a good long-term investment. There was no better time for making such purchases as in the recession of the 1930s when prices were at a low ebb. David A. Randall, Librarian of the Lilly Library, has recorded how, when he learned that Fleming had lost interest in continuing with the collection, he attempted to purchase it. No date for this approach is given, but Randall's comment was that 'the wily Fleming preferred to let it sit in a London depository as a hedge against inflation. In this he was right'.[5] After Fleming's death the books were left in trust for his son. Eventually, through the offices of Percy Muir, they came to Indiana University, as also did the original manuscripts of the James Bond Books.

One of Fleming's great interests at this time (one very typical of his fondness for new gadgets of all kinds) was in the work of Charles Babbage, who in many ways was the inventor of the computer 150 years prior to its production. When the second centenary of Babbage's birth was celebrated at the South Kensington Science Museum in 1991, the staff set out to reconstruct the world's first computer in order to demonstrate that Babbage's 'Second Difference Engine' could have been built 150 years earlier if the government of the day had not ceased to fund it. Many scientists believed that Britain would have won a great industrial advantage if the machine had been finished then. Professor Isaac Asimov went so far as to say that 'later versions of it might have shortened the task of winning the First World War'.[6]

Babbage was just the type of character to have attracted Fleming's interest. In 1812 he founded the Analytical Society, 'for promoting the principles of pure D-ism in opposition to the Dotage of the university' (he was referring to Cambridge). His range of subjects extended from submarines, lighthouses, archaeology and lock-picking to deciphering. Babbage's papers on a variety of subjects are in the Manuscripts Department of the British Museum, where they were carefully studied by Fleming. What fascinated him particularly were the papers on deciphering, which Babbage compared to 'the picking of locks'.

It may well have been that Fleming's interest was particularly aroused because Babbage seems to have become a detective of nineteenth-century love affairs, as his papers fully reveal. He was frequently consulted by all manner of people, from cabinet ministers and lawyers seeking information on how to solve divorce cases to frantic parents trying to find solutions to the coded love messages of their children. For this was the age of furtive and coded love messages, which appeared daily in *The Times* and other newspapers. Much later Fleming wrote a paper on Babbage's work in the field of cryptography. It was later submitted to Naval Intelligence, but no copy of it seems to have been kept.

However, he seems to have tried to find new uses for his study of cryptography, because in 1936, after he had left Reuters, he approached that news agency again to discuss a service that offered 'to carry coded telegrams between London and New York at 3.6 pence per word as against the existing cable rate of $5\frac{1}{2}$ pence per word'. This project was stopped, however, because of a clause in the International Telegraph Regulations.

Many years later when I was discussing with Fleming the possibility of my writing a history of British secret services down the ages, he said to me: 'Do you know who the first "C" was?' Naturally I replied: 'Mansfield Cumming.' 'Wrong. The first "C" was a chap called Charles Babbage, who used the letter "C" as a pseudonym in his correspondence with his inner circle. We had no proper official secret service then, but Babbage is worth studying because he paved the way for improved codes and ciphers.' Fleming went on to say that when Babbage had been let down by the British Government in the funding of his analytical machine he went to Italy in the middle of the last century to try to get it produced there. Quite casually, Fleming added: 'During the war I tried to find out whether by any chance the Italians had resurrected the scheme, but the answer seemed to be "no".' By this time, of course, work on the first complete computer was being carried out between the American Professor Howard Aiken and the IBM Company. Fleming then mentioned that *Passages from the Life of a Philosopher* by Babbage, published in 1864, was 'one of the most cherished in my collection'.

As I have already mentioned, Fleming's interests were very diverse and probably this was one of the reasons he took so long to find the right career for himself. Even now it is evident that he succeeded in three careers: in Intelligence, in journalism and as a novelist. One of the secrets of how he managed to maintain so many interests and also, let it be stressed, to keep some of them absolutely secret except to the few, was the way in which he developed his friendships. 'The male friends were kept . . . in compartments,' comments Ivar Bryce regarding Fleming's capacity for friendship.

To some extent this applied to women as well, particularly those with whom he remained on terms of friendship for many years. Perhaps his best friendships with women were those he kept strictly private. Though he belonged to clubs, he did not confine his men friends to club members, as so many used to do. By avoiding too many parties and social chit-chat he allowed himself time to have many individual friends in all walks of life. He much preferred a lunch or dinner with one person than with half a dozen. In terms of gathering information, such tactics paid off.

In the City he made a number of friends without ever enjoying the life there. One of his colleagues, Hugh Vivian-Smith, has been quoted as saying that 'as a stockbroker old Ian really must have been among the world's worst'.[7] I think the truth was that he regarded dabbling in stocks and shares as gambling and never took it very seriously. His advice to me was that the soundest form of saving in the long term was to buy the right kind of books. He even told me what to buy and how long to hold them before selling. 'H.G. Wells first editions are now very, very cheap,' he said in the 1950s. 'Buy now and sell in, say, ten years time to America and you should easily quadruple your output.' I did and he was right.

By this time Fleming had set up home at 22A Ebury Street, on the borders of fashionable Belgravia and the more plebeian Pimlico. It was a somewhat dilapidated house when he took it over. This is hardly surprising, as it had previously been used as a chapel, a school and a warehouse. One of the first visitors to his new home was Vanessa Hoffmann from Germany. It was at her suggestion that he engaged a German interior decorator to make changes to his abode. 'Far enough away from Fitzrovia, close enough to Bohemian Chelsea and within reasonable distance of the City' was how Fleming once described it. Most of his entertaining was done here, but, once again, he divided his guests up according to his respective interests: an antiquarian book collector on his own, three bridge-playing friends on another occasion, someone from the City one night and certain girls in rotation at other times. On the other hand he did create what could be called the Fleming circle and he actually called it *Le Cercle* – a group of friends, some of them Old Etonians, who gathered for parties at 22A Ebury Street once or twice a month. Most of *Le Cercle* were bridge- or golf-playing associates. None of them belonged to the shooting and hunting fraternity, for whom Fleming seemed to have no time at all. One of his closest friends and one who helped him form *Le Cercle* was Gerald Coke, who later became Chairman of the Glyndebourne Arts Trust, a director of the Royal Academy of Music and a governor of the BBC as well as having a directorship with the Rio Tinto-Zinc Corporation.

One of Fleming's golf-playing friends was Lord O'Neill, who married Anne Charteris, many years later to become Fleming's wife. Fleming first met Anne at Le Touquet in August 1935, and from then onwards he was a frequent visitor to her home. However, in those days of the late thirties he was perfectly content with his bachelor existence and had no thoughts about marriage. His mother had convinced him that it would be wise to remain single for some time to come. Nevertheless he continued to keep in touch with Vanessa Hoffmann, whom he had looked up more than once when working for Reuters in Germany. There were certain special reasons for maintaining a close relationship with Vanessa, even if they were far apart. She had important contacts with leading Germans, including Admiral Wilhelm Canaris, who was head of the *Abwehr*, the German Secret Service. She had also interested Fleming in the fact that a number of leading Nazis were involved in occult practices and relied a great deal on astrological predictions.

Marigold Kilpatrick, who knew both Ian and Vanessa when she was studying in Munich, says: 'Vanessa was one of the few women whom Ian treated almost as one of his male friends – like an equal. Vanessa had the most extraordinary interests and Ian seemed delighted to discuss them with her. We called them the Two-person Seminar. I think Ian regarded astrology originally as something of a joke, but Vanessa convinced him that it was vitally important if one needed to assess people's character.'

From remarks Fleming made later in life it seems he shared this view, even though he may have put it over in a joking way. He may also have been influenced in occult literature through having met Carl Jung, who had written a foreword to Richard Wilhelm's translation of *I Ching*, the Chinese *Book of Changes*. What is significant, especially in relation to his women friends, is that he and they always seemed to exchange information on what sign of the zodiac they were born under. This will be evident as the story of Fleming progresses. On the other hand Fleming himself would have been one of the first to dismiss any total commitment to astrology as being 'right over the top', to cite one of his frequent phrases when he wished to stress the need for caution on some subject or other.

In the late thirties his friendships and acquaintanceships ranged from Fitzrovia to Chelsea. Augustus John, who had painted his mother and who later did a splendid sketch of Fleming, was all his life one of his heroes. He saw Augustus as a kind of uncrowned king of Fitzrovia, which in many respects he undoubtedly was. Yet another acquaintance was Aleister Crowley, the man so often and somewhat unfairly referred to as 'The Great Beast'. Crowley, after a university education at Cambridge, had spent a fortune on research into the occult at the time of the 'magic revival' of the late nineteenth century. He became a member of the Golden Dawn Order and later founded his own order, the Silver Star. A practitioner of yoga, he was also a mountaineer, having climbed K2, the second highest mountain in the world. Somerset Maugham had used Crowley as the model for Oliver Haddo in his book *The Magician*. Crowley was not amused by this.

Aleister Crowley played a considerable part in one period of Fleming's life. In the sphere of the occult he was as fascinating as was Augustus John in the world of painters. In the First World War he had indulged in pro-German propaganda, writing for Vierveck in *The Fatherland* and *The International*, which he edited for about a year. Crowley himself always claimed that he did so merely to ingratiate himself with the Germans in order that he could spy on them. The American Intelligence Service seem to have believed Crowley's story, though the British NID rejected him, and his occult temple in London was closed down by the police on some pretext or other.

Fleming was usually prepared to listen to the other side of an argument and in the case of Crowley he seems to have done so. His contacts with 'the Great Magician' continued until the war years when Crowley was living in Jermyn Street. Crowley's adopted son, Amado, tells me that 'Fleming always addressed my father as "Master" and talked to me as if I were a prince and he was my private detective. In other words there seemed to be a sort of deference. This, together with one or two other hints, leads me to think he might well have seen himself as Crowley's student.'[8]

Just how open-minded Fleming was at that time may be judged from the fact that he had a job in the City. Perhaps Fitzrovia and Chelsea were ways of escape from his work, which he undoubtedly disliked. After the First World War Crowley was almost prosecuted for his alleged activities in helping the enemy, but it was eventually proved that he had genuinely intended to help the Allies. What clinched the decision to exonerate him was his revelation that the international head of the Hermetic sect which he joined was in fact a highly dangerous German agent and Crowley had revealed this to the Americans. In the inter-war years Crowley spent a great deal of time in Berlin and supplied British Intelligence with information on continental communism. The German intelligence service certainly knew all about Crowley's ventures in espionage, as Crowley lived in Berlin with another notorious spy, Gerald Hamilton. Crowley was spying on Hamilton for MI5, while Hamilton was almost certainly spying on Crowley for the Germans. Living together as friends, they concocted reports on one another.

Whether or not yet another war with Germany was inevitable was a prime question in the late thirties and it was a subject that Fleming began to study carefully. He had his own contacts in Germany quite apart from Vanessa Hoffmann, but he relied heavily on any information she was able to pass on to him. Fully realizing from such reports that Germany's armed forces would be invincible in the event of war, he felt the only realistic choice that faced Britain was to win allies inside Germany, in other words men with sufficient influence either to supersede Hitler or to turn him away from ideas of world conquest. Gradually it dawned on him that the one man who might just fill this role was Admiral Canaris. Other information which made Fleming feel sure that Canaris was the man to deal with came from Ian Colvin, at that time stationed in Berlin as a correspondent for the *News*

*Chronicle*. In 1938 Colvin was informed of a talk between Fabian von Schlabrendorff, who was a contact between Canaris and Dr Schacht, in which Canaris had said: 'Don't forget, we have not talked treason – only discussed the safety of the Reich.' This conversation, Colvin learned, was about a suggestion that together Canaris and Schlabrendorff could work with the British Secret Service against Hitler. But, warned Canaris, 'should you work for them [the British SIS] it will most probably be brought to my notice, as I think I have penetrated it here and there'.[9]

Yet another of Fleming's contacts on Germany was Karl Heinz Abshagen, a German journalist who in 1938 was stationed in London, and who later wrote a biography of Canaris. How much of this information Fleming passed on to Establishment figures is still not clear, but he was in touch with Sir Robert Vansittart of the Foreign Office from time to time. It may well have been that Vansittart had encouraged Fleming's somewhat sudden and mysterious visit to Moscow again early in 1939. Officially, he was sent as a representative of *The Times*, though this was in fact a cover for his making some inquiries for the Foreign Office. His reports back to *The Times* were short and relatively insignificant: he was in Moscow for only a few days. During this trip he made the acquaintance of Sefton Delmer, the *Daily Express* correspondent, later to become a colleague in British Intelligence. As they left Russia in the Warsaw Express, Delmer, dreading the intense censorship in border-crossing from the USSR, memorized his notes and then tore them up and threw them away. Fleming teased him mockingly: 'Why don't you swallow them? That's what all the best spies do.' When they reached the Polish frontier their luggage was searched thoroughly by the border guards, Delmer's fairly casually but Fleming's in great detail. In Fleming's luggage they discovered a carton of contraceptives made of Russian synthetic latex which Fleming was carrying back to London to be chemically analyzed. Delmer recorded that the Russians held each sample to the light and examined it and he commented to Fleming: 'You should have swallowed them.'[10]

People who knew Ian Fleming in this period report on his light-heartedness and flippancy more than anything else. He tended to be more masterful in his relations with British girls than he had been with the continentals. 'English girls need to be shown one is master of one's destiny,' he used to say. Another of his phrases which nobody could quite explain was: 'If you want a husband, you should go to the Baltic Exchange.' Yet another phrase of his to describe a crowd of both sexes was 'the clustered and the cleft'. Probably this was a phrase picked up in his school-days at Eton. I recall Oliver Lyttelton (the late Lord Chandos), also an Old Etonian, telling me that this was a comment made by Queen Elizabeth I which he had learned at school. At parties Fleming danced only occasionally, but when he made his first visit to New York in the thirties he became very fond of the night-spots of Harlem and used to dance rather more when in that vicinity.

There have been various accounts of exactly how Ian Fleming was recruited into the Royal Navy's Intelligence Division shortly be-fore the Second World War began. A number of people were consulted and Fleming was recommended by both Sir Maurice (later Lord) Hankey and Sir Edward Peacock. However, without doubt the original recommendation that carried most weight came from the formidable Sir Montagu (later Lord) Norman, Governor of the Bank of England.[11] This much is clear from what Rear-Admiral John Godfrey, Director of Naval Intelligence at the time, noted in May 1939: 'Norman rang up and said: "We've found your man."' A few days later Admiral Godfrey, Admiral Aubrey Hugh-Smith, Angus Macdonnell and Fleming met for lunch at the old Carlton Hotel Grill. At the end of August that year Fleming was commissioned as a lieutenant, RNVR, Special Branch.

It has been suggested that Fleming had never met Norman, but the late Paul Einzig, one of Norman's biographers, assures me that they had met before Norman made his recommendation. 'Norman would never have given such a firm recommendation for an important post without having seen the man personally. After all, this was not the case of recruiting another lieutenant for the NID but of finding a man who would make the ideal personal assistant for the DNI. Norman never relied solely on other people's suggestions. You must remember, too, that Norman kept his own personal mini-intelligence service. In that sense he was unlike any other governor of the Bank of England before or since. From what I learned from Norman himself it was clear that Fleming had been one of his occasional informants long before the war. What had impressed Norman most when he first met Fleming was the interesting parallels in their own two careers. Both men were Old Etonians and both had the reputation for being rebels when at school. Fleming had failed to get into Oxford, while Norman's sudden departure from King's College, Cambridge, after one year was because of a disagreement with his director of studies. He had been told that he was of no use and wouldn't get a degree. Finally, and this is the most remarkable coincidence in the two men's lives, while Fleming went to Switzerland, Austria and Germany to learn languages after failing at Sandhurst, Norman left King's to go to Dresden to learn German and to Switzerland to learn French. Thus the parallels in their early careers were of special interest to Norman. There is no doubt that he was impressed by Fleming's wide range of contacts from people in the City and especially in Germany and such odd types as Dennis Wheatley and Aleister Crowley.'[12]

In the early days of the Second World War it had been the custom of the Director of Naval Intelligence of that era, the celebrated Admiral Sir Reginald Hall, to fill key posts in his service from stockbrokers and people in the City. Thus when Rear-Admiral (later Sir John) Godfrey was appointed the new DNI early in 1939 with the prospect of war distinctly imminent, it was not unnatural that he should follow tradition in this respect. Indeed, he was recommended to do so by Hall himself. As to the role of the Governor of the Bank of England in all this, there is no doubt that Norman understood much about the gathering of intelligence and that his own network of informants around the world was quite considerable. Norman rather delighted in being mysterious himself: he loved to travel incognito, using such names as 'Mr Collet' and 'Professor Skinner' in doing so.

Apart from Fleming there were other new entries to the NID from the City, including the barrister Rodger Winn, who ended up as head of the U-Boat Tracking Room. Godfrey had an enormous task in front of him, that of repairing years of neglect inside the NID and he set about it by recruiting many talented civilians. Over the next three years the staff of the NID was expanded tenfold.

Room 39 in the NID was reached by the Admiralty door which opened to the Mall, being close to No. 10 Downing Street, the Foreign Office and Horse Guards. This was the office occupied by Admiral Godfrey, just as Room 40 had been the number of that occupied by Hall in the First World War. Maybe the number was changed from 40 to 39 for security purposes, as the very name of 'Room 40' had become well known by overseas intelligence services long before. It was in Room 39 that Godfrey held his morning conferences. Fleming was stationed at a desk close to the door of this office so as to be within instant call of his chief, and was given the title of Personal Assistant to the DNI.

From the very beginning Fleming decided exactly how *he* intended himself to be regarded in this department. While some might argue that it was not for a mere personal assistant to make such a decision, the reality was that to be an effective PA he needed to set certain standards of his own from the outset. This was not a mere PA's job: Fleming was required to use his own initiative and on occasions to make decisions of his own. More importantly, he had to liaise with key people, including the head of the Secret Service, or MI6 as it was designated. He had been well briefed by Sir Montagu Norman on Godfrey the man; he knew that Godfrey was a demanding chief and one whose temper was on a short fuse. So from the start of his appointment he made it clear that he was not one to be pushed around, that he treated senior officers no differently from any civilians, even to the extent of declining to call them 'Sir'. He would not hesitate to argue against a senior officer if he thought that officer was wrong.

Few young men of the age of thirty-one, as Fleming then was, would have dared to take such a line. That he did so and actually succeeded in making himself highly respected and trusted, winning Godfrey's full approval, is a tribute to the ability of the man. It is especially remarkable when one bears in mind that he had never previously held any administrative post. The late Donald McLachlan said of him:

If not the wisest of the staff in Room 39 who operated day by day on behalf of the Director, Ian Fleming was the most vivid and became the best-known personality. His gift was much less for the analysis and weighing of intelligence than for running things and for drafting. He was a skilled fixer and vigorous showman, and he seemed to transmit the energy and wide-ranging curiosity of his first chief by whom so much was delegated. Never, as a colleague put it, did Fleming 'sleep with a problem'. He would throw out the hint of a solution or initiate immediate action.[13]

As noted earlier, Fleming's code-name was 17F. Here Fleming's flirtations with the occult and astrology in particular caused him to comment to one or two colleagues that 'in numerology No. 17 is a fortunate one. It is linked to divination and prophecy and the principles of truth, hope and faith as well as being linked to my astronomical birth sign of Gemini'.[14]

It was in the NID that Fleming renewed his acquaintance with William Plomer, who was later to help find him a publisher. Plomer, another civilian recruited into the NID, had been a reader and adviser for Jonathan Cape. Well known as a poet, he was also the discoverer and editor of what became known as *Kilvert's Diary*, the musings of a country clergyman, which was published in 1938–40. Referring to Ian's work in the NID, Plomer said:

> He was an unfailing source of brilliant and constructive ideas, and he had the faculty of knowing how to apply them in a practical way. Also, in a service traditionally silent, and sometimes tongue-tied, he was notably articulate both in conversation and on paper . . . there were times when the risk of giving offence was nothing compared with the importance of being, if necessary, blunt.[15]

Promotion to lieutenant-commander followed fairly swiftly as Godfrey recognized the value of his PA. Godfrey was astute enough to realize that he desperately needed someone who could at times act as an intermediary with other branches of Intelligence, while at the same time sorting out difficult situations and smoothing down potentially damaging disputes on policy.

Admiral Sir Norman Denning, who at that time was Paymaster Lieutenant-Commander serving in the NID, has testified to Fleming's ability in coping with such problems: 'Ian had enormous flair, imagination and ability to get on with people . . . he was perfect for the job. He could fix anyone or anything, if it was really necessary.'[16]

Tact and a knack of turning an awkward situation into something to laugh about were essential qualifications in the kind of office chores with which Ian had to cope. Inevitably there were clashes between the views of regular service officers and the more open-minded new civilian intake, not to mention disagreements between the NID chiefs and some of the senior Admiralty officers. Often Fleming would take the brunt of these, using his ability to make a joke at the right moment when discussions became tense and on other occasions being tersely ruthless. He would even dare to intercept a message for the DNI and send it back to the originator with the refutation: 'No importance – 17F'. Few other personal assistants would even consider taking such action without showing such a message to their chiefs first of all.

Matters were not helped in the early days of the war by the fact that Winston Churchill was then First Lord of the Admiralty, as he had been briefly in the First World War. Godfrey and Churchill were soon in disagreement over a variety of matters. The former wanted all intelligence reports to be properly and scientifically analysed before they were accepted, whereas Churchill in the early stages of the war found this time-wasting. Early in the war Churchill refused to accept the DNI's figures of U-boats sunk and broadcast his own grossly exaggerated version of submarines sunk by the Royal Navy. Matters came to a head when, on 20 January 1940, Churchill indulged in some wishful-thinking propaganda that belied the facts. He made a broadcast in which he alleged that 'half the U-boats with which Germany began the war have been sunk, and their new building has fallen behind what we expected'.

This was a half-truth translated into a dangerous optimism. The British Admiralty, it is true, had been misled before the war into believing that the Germans had more U-boats than in fact existed and it took some time for the NID to change this viewpoint. Even so the NID never shared Churchill's publicly declared opinion in this period. There was a marked controversy between the NID and Churchill on this subject in early 1940 and in the reports of the DNI to the Chief of Naval Staff this was fully reflected, most notably in the statement – for which Fleming was at least in part responsible – that it would be 'most unwise optimistically to assume that the Germans will lose fifty-two U-boats in the next six months'.

Lt-Commander Patrick Beesly, RNVR, another member of the NID at the time, told the author: 'There is no doubt whatsoever that Godfrey's figures were right and those Churchill gave were wrong. What made things even more difficult was that Churchill adamantly banned the circulation of the reports of our Assessment Committee to anyone on the Naval Staff or in the Fleet other than himself and the Vice-Chief of Naval Staff.'[17]

Churchill was then anxious to reassert his authority, doubtless already having his mind on possibly becoming Prime Minister before the war developed into full-scale action. To try to achieve this he sought publicity for himself even if it meant publishing untrue and exaggerated accounts of U-boat sinkings. His hostility to Godfrey never ended. Not only did he make life difficult for the DNI with the Joint Intelligence Council, but he tried to pave the way for Godfrey's removal, while at the end of the war it was surely largely due to Churchill that Godfrey was the only officer of his rank to receive no official recognition of his services in the Allied cause.

Indeed the relationship between Godfrey and Churchill was so difficult that the DNI frequently used Fleming as a useful intermediary in drafting replies to the First Sea Lord. Godfrey had such confidence in Fleming's judgement that he used him as a liaison officer not only with the wartime heads of the Secret Service but with the Special Operations Executive (which co-operated with Resistance movements in Europe) and the Political Warfare Executive. Fleming was also given a free hand in establishing contacts of his own and even in doing a certain amount of lone-hand espionage. In an account of the work of PA to the DNI, which he wrote in 1948, Fleming stated that the PA 'was also a convenient channel for confidential matters connected with subversive organizations, and for undertaking confidential missions abroad, either alone or with the DNI. . . . It is recommended that such an appointment should be created in any future war'.

This is an admirable summary of how Fleming personally shaped the job of PA. It was a tremendous and, to his friends, an unexpected achievement. A colleague of his in the NID, Robert Harling, says that Fleming's friends decided that the job 'was highly inappropriate to his true talents and would drive him mad on several counts within a month . . . the job would mean being polite to the pompous and kind to the crass, and here again Fleming was ill-equipped by character or inclination for such dedication to the State. . . . To the surprise of many, and to the utter perplexity of his friends, Fleming took these demands in his stride, meeting them ably and equably'.[18]

One of the main reasons that Fleming made such a success of the job was that from the start he enjoyed working for Godfrey. Both men were inclined to be impatient and wanted swift action. Yet another reason may well have been Fleming's personal long-held aim of trying to win Admiral Canaris over to the Allied side. This was an aim he quietly pursued in a somewhat secretive manner, not altogether surprising because for some few years before the war the NID paid little attention to Canaris in his new role as chief of the *Abwehr*. Nevertheless he had very little help officially regarding Canaris, as the Admiralty took the somewhat unimaginative view that, since Canaris was no longer associated with the German Navy, inquiries concerning him were best left to MI6.

In one respect Godfrey was slow and stubborn in coming to terms with technological developments in the sphere of code-cracking. While both the Army and the RAF had shown instant and enthusiastic interest in 'Ultra', the code-breaking project at Bletchley Park, Buckinghamshire, Godfrey's reaction had been tepid, to put it mildly. He upheld the outdated view that the NID was the senior Intelligence Service and a law unto itself. Yet Bletchley had broken the German naval Enigma ciphers and Group Captain Winterbotham of the Ultra team wrote that, despite this,

I knew it would not have been any good trying to get John Godfrey, the D.N.I., to come in earlier. He wasn't at all keen even now . . . I managed to persuade him to send one naval officer to join the party at Bletchley . . . the D.N.I. insisted that the naval signals should still go to the Admiralty in the original German, notwithstanding the fact that those concerning the U-boat traffic or German ship movements were already being translated and being sent to Coastal Command of the R.A.F.[19]

This attitude robbed Ultra of much of its efficiency regarding the Navy in the early stages of the war, and Marshal of the RAF Sir John Slessor referred to the fact that 'characteristically and not always with happy results, the Admiralty were allowed to keep these signal Intelligence matters in their own hands'.[20]

# 3

# Operation Danube

... the Admiralty recognized the importance of the Danube
very early indeed, not only in itself, but in conjunction with
the Romanian oil wells, both so vital to the German
economy. . . . But it is Ian Fleming who is and must be the
central figure.[1]

Q uite often Fleming would undertake missions of his own
quite independently of the Admiralty. Sometimes these
concerned other branches of Intelligence. On occasions such missions included passing on ideas to his friend, Dennis Wheatley,
the writer, who had written his own, unofficial and highly original
ideas for repelling a German invasion. As a result, Wheatley had
been installed in Churchill's secret underground fortress off
Whitehall, being the only civilian member of the Joint Planning
Staff. 'I had quite a number of dealings with Fleming when I was
in the War Cabinet Offices,' wrote Wheatley. 'He was full of ideas
not only for helping to stop the invasion, but for our eventual
plans to land on the continent.'[2]

Both Wheatley and Fleming studied the prospects and even
worked out a plan for invading Sardinia rather than Sicily. Each
believed that such a course would shorten the war appreciably.
That the plan was considered on high is clear, documents reveal-
ing that it was named Operation Brimstone. Eisenhower is said to
have been keen on the project, but it was turned down by the
Chief of Staff, Sir Alan Brooke.

Fleming and Wheatley were afterwards involved together in some
of the planning for Operation Mincemeat, one of the most successful deception operations of the war. This was the somewhat
ghoulish code-word for the 'man who never was', the fictitious

major of the Royal Marines whose corpse was jettisoned from a
British submarine off the coast of Spain and allowed to drift
ashore. The Spaniards recovered the body and, as British Intelligence guessed, passed on the information to the Germans. That
'information' was contained in documents placed in a brief-case
(chained to his person), intended to mislead the Germans into
believing that the Allied landings would come in the Eastern
Mediterranean and Sardinia rather than Sicily. The NID played a
major role in this ploy and Fleming's contacts inside Spain were
vital to its success. It was Fleming's friend, the attractive, lively
and gregarious Don Gomez-Beare, whose principal area of operations was Gibraltar but who travelled far and wide in Spain, who
was sent post-haste to Huelva, near where the body of 'Major
Martin' was floated ashore. His role was to contact the Spanish
authorities and, in order to play up the importance of what was in
the brief-case, to hint to them that the major was carrying vital
papers which must not fall into the hands of the Germans. He
made it clear that he was not asking for the papers, but only that
they should be kept from the Germans. These tactics worked, as
Gomez-Beare was certain they would: pro-Germans among the
Spaniards allowed the Germans not only to see the papers but to
photograph them before they were handed over to the British.

When in the early summer of 1940 various roundabout communications arrived in Whitehall, suggesting that an invasion of
Britain was imminent, it was suspected that some of these were
instigated by Goebbels's propaganda department. One such message, supposed to have come from a German agent, told of plans
for an attack on Southend by parachute troops. This was taken
sufficiently seriously for some precautions to be taken in Southend
by the military. Ian Fleming took the view that it was essential
that there should be an official monitoring the proposed attack so
that any attempt by Goebbels to make propaganda out of it could
instantly be refuted. In his biography of Peter Fleming, Duff
Hart-Davis tells how Peter and his brother Ian 'found themselves
going down to Southend on the afternoon of Whit Saturday in a
camouflaged staff car. Expecting to find deserted streets and tanks
behind bathing machines, they saw instead a seaside resort in full
bank holiday swing'.

The brothers Fleming kept watch from a naval observation post that had been set up in Southend and waited until long after nightfall. Nothing happened, however, and they returned to London. This is yet another example of how often in the Intelligence field frustration seems prevalent; it also shows how the two brothers often co-operated in such exercises, despite the still repeated stories of some that they did not get along together.

Frustration was a regular feature of life in the NID in the early days of the war. One severe blow to that organization was the Venlo Incident. In November 1939 two British Secret Service agents, Captain Payne Best and Major Richard Stevens, set out on a mission which, they optimistically hoped, would end the war. Their mission was to meet an allegedly high-ranking German officer whose name they did not know, but who, some in London thought, might be Admiral Canaris. Lured by car to Venlo on the Dutch–German border, they were kidnapped by German Intelligence agents, with the result that the British Secret Service network in Europe was compromised in a single afternoon. The NID was affected because as a result of this operation the Germans learned the identity of one of the most highly prized informants to the British on German naval secrets: Otto Kreuger, a naval engineering consultant.

Some long time after the Venlo incident the NID learned that the Germans had been reading much of the Royal Navy's signals traffic. Such news, however, came too late to prevent some of the disasters of the Norwegian campaign which were partly due to this very factor. It soon became clear that, following their interrogations of Best and Stevens, the Germans had even penetrated some NID secrets. News reached Fleming that Canaris was extremely worried about the Venlo episode. The Admiral, though head of the *Abwehr*, had not organized this particular operation and he was afraid that Best and Stevens might have discovered links that he had himself established with the British.

One naval operator who had consequently been identified was Commander Frank Alexander Slocum, who had joined MI6 in 1937. Later he was brought back to work under NID orders to operate what was in effect a private navy for espionage purposes.[3]

Such sudden shocks as the amount of valuable intelligence the

Germans gleaned about British operations after Venlo convinced the NID of the need to increase what until then had been their very modest Contacts Register. Fleming entered into this work with great gusto. He brought in contacts of his own and even launched a dinner party at the Savoy to create a panel of patrons for the Register. Those invited to participate ranged from Lloyds and Hambros Banks to various oil companies. By the end of the war the Contacts Register totalled more than seventy thousand names, much of the credit for which must go to Fleming. Apart from bringing banking and commercial firms into this service, he had imaginatively chosen many individual contacts in North America and the Caribbean.

David Herbert, Fleming's friend from Eton, was himself engaged in secret operations on behalf of the British at this time. Fleming soon contacted him and arranged a number of missions for Herbert, which involved co-operating with spies inside the French fishing fleets. 'It was largely a case of sending French spies across the seas and bringing back tired ones,' David Herbert says.

In these early months of the war Fleming was at times irked by the fact that his was mainly a desk job and he became more and more determined to associate himself with some direct action against the enemy. In the early winter of 1939–40 he was a prime instigator in a plan to try to block the Danube to German ships. Diligent and enthusiastic pressure on his part persuaded Admiral Godfrey to support the initiation of a number of clandestine operations aimed at not only blocking the Danube but crippling the Romanian oil refineries and briefing double agents to take part in these schemes. The project, which involved a small team of officers temporarily attached to the NID, was named Operation Danube.

It was perhaps originally too ambitious a scheme and extremely complicated in its aims. Fleming's undercover team was dispatched to Bucharest, charged with closing the Germans' principal oil lifeline from the Black Sea by blocking the Iron Gates, some twenty-five miles of dangerous narrows in the Danube between Romania and Yugoslavia. The Danube was to be blocked with sunken barges. It is still not quite clear if this plan had full and detailed clearance from the Cabinet, but Sir Robert Bellairs, co-ordinator of Intelligence to the Cabinet, was informed about it. Officially, details of the project have never been admitted, though doubtless they are tucked away in certain secret files. It has been reported that many signals and records of naval affairs were destroyed shortly after the end of the war. Surprisingly, it has been admitted that 'some duplicates can be found in the National Archives in Washington, but may be still classified if the British say so'.[4]

Fleming chose for this operation three men of widely different talents. Appointed as Assistant Naval Attaché, Belgrade, was Alexander Glen, a young RNVR officer educated at Fettes and Balliol College, Oxford, who had been leader of three Oxford University Arctic expeditions between 1932 and 1936. Secondly, and the senior member of the team in age, there was Lt-Commander Michael Mason, a first-class shot and an amateur boxer of some distinction who, after Eton and Sandhurst, found himself in the Second World War in the Navy, not the Army. He was sufficiently adaptable to fill all kinds of roles from intelligence operative to commander of a landing-craft flotilla. According to *Who's Who*, he had spent a great deal of his life travelling extensively, 'mostly in wild places' and he had also been Commodore of the Royal Ocean Racing Club. During 1942–3 I served under Michael Mason and found him a most courageous officer.

The third choice was perhaps the least satisfactory, though justifiable on the grounds of previous service and experience. He was Lt-Commander Merlin Minshall, yet another RNVR officer. Like Mason, he was a first-class shot. A racing motorist before the war, he had also been a karate expert and had been mixed up in some daring escapades among Nazi agents. Some of his enemies dubbed Minshall 'a bloody pirate', and he loved to play the role of the secret agent of fiction, a role that became somewhat of a fixation for him as time went on. Indeed, later in life he claimed without justification that Fleming had based the character of James Bond on him. In newspaper and radio interviews in February 1977, Minshall said of Fleming: 'He was ruthless, unsure of himself and a romantic. All the qualities that I had, he wished he had. That's why he used me as his model for Bond.'

This extravagantly inventive raconteur also claimed that his mother, Theodora Wigham-Richardson, had been a successful spy in the 1914–18 war and that she taught him 'the tactics of the trade'.[5] He also told anyone who would listen that he was kidnapped by the Gestapo in 1939, but that he escaped and made his way home disguised as a doctor on the last Orient Express train before war broke out. As far as Operation Danube was concerned, Michael Mason told me that 'Minshall was a disaster throughout. On one occasion in Glen's presence I had to knock him out to save us all from trouble.'

Certainly Minshall knew the area well, which was the main reason why he was chosen for Operation Danube. He had actually travelled along the River Danube in a Dutch barge before the war, narrowly escaping death by poisoning at the hands of a beautiful female Nazi agent, according to his own account of the affair. Certainly he knew how to put himself over as the most daring of agents.

When Minshall arrived in Bucharest to help launch this operation he had with him false-bottomed suitcases carrying detonators and high explosives disguised with the red and gold foil of Mackintosh's toffee de luxe, while gelignite was to be shipped out in a diplomatic bag. Minshall told how, having failed to bribe the Iron Gates pilots with gold sovereigns, he commandeered half a dozen British ships lying in Braila harbour and then had a crew of British ratings brought out from Britain to man them.

He claimed that he got his convoy out of the harbour only after surviving two attempts to kill him by means of poison being put in his wine. But, as a result of the Germans siphoning fuel out of his boats under cover of night, the vessels ran dry before they reached the Iron Gates and were halted. Minshall said he escaped arrest by evading the convoy in a naval launch which was following, adding that he filled the launch with explosives and rammed it at high speed into the railway embankment.

This somewhat muddled and not altogether comprehensible story of his part in Operation Danube has been disputed both by Lt-Commander Mason and Sir Alexander Glen. Mason stated that the initial project was to blow up the Romanian banks of the river at the Iron Gates so that they would be impassable for German barges. This plan, he added, was ruined as a result of another agent talking too much and, in desperation, some thirteen tons of gelignite were shipped out to Bucharest in 1940 on the Orient Express through Italy, the cases of the explosive being labelled as the ambassador's luggage. Mason also claimed that while he was working with another agent, a Romanian, he had to deal with two men who had been watching him in the dining-car of the Orient Express. 'I knew they'd be waiting to jump me in the corridor and there they were. I hit one under the heart and one in the jaw and out they went. I beat them insensible and threw them off through the lavatory window.'[6]

Though this operation was not a success, Fleming learned a great deal from it. Sir Alexander Glen paid this tribute to Fleming in connection with the Danube Operation:

> . . . certainly the Admiralty recognized the importance of the Danube very early indeed, not only in itself, but in conjunction with the Romanian oil wells, both so vital to the German economy. . . . Captain Max Despard, whose assistant I was [as assistant naval attaché in Belgrade at the time], played a vital part in planning both operations. But it is Ian Fleming who is and must be the central figure. . . . Michael Mason had physical and mental attributes which would have stretched Bond at his very best. . . . Dunstan Curtis had a part – elegance and courage in a nicely understatement way. . . . But much of Bond lay in Fleming himself, in his own sharp mind, his imagination and his frustrations, too, at being tied so often to a desk job as the D.N.I.'s personal assistant.[7]

Yet out of these early failures came triumphant success in the end. A small force, led by Major Rostham and Major Greenwood, entered the Iron Gates sector in 1943–4, as a result of which a number of tugs and barges were sunk. Admiral Sir John Cunningham and Air Chief Marshal Sir John Slessor had perceived accurately the significance of the Danube to the supply of the *Wehrmacht*, especially in the Caucasus and rather later for the evacuation of German forces from the Crimea. With the help of HMS *Vernon* and the technical skill of the Fleet Torpedo Officer, Mediterranean, a particularly lethal combination of acoustic and magnetic mines was designed and built. These were dropped at low level at night by

Liberator and Wellington aircraft during a concentrated programme of some months, achieving devastating results.

Monitoring the effect on the Danube with the Partisan forces was the same Commander Glen whom Fleming had sent to Belgrade four years earlier. To strengthen the link with Fleming throughout this prolonged operation, a Royal Navy minesweeping force was held in readiness at Istanbul to clear the river for Soviet use as and when necessary. This was under the command of Captain Vladimir Wolfson, RNVR. But welcome as this force was for the Soviet Commander-in-Chief of the Third Ukrainian Army, Marshal Tolbukhan, Moscow gave a terse 'no' to its employment. As an outcome of this stubbornness, the Soviet advance towards Budapest was to suffer delays and casualties which Wolfson's minesweepers could have done much to minimize.

'Fleming's private self – or selves, because he was not a man of a single interest or a single aspect – seemed to some to be hidden or withdrawn,' said William Plomer. 'There were persons near him during the war who felt that they never really knew him except as an active functionary, polite and often cheerful with those who seemed to him properly tuned up, and capable of being abrupt with others.'[8]

The main characteristic of the PA to the DNI was that he was never short of ideas. They poured out of him with almost every development of the war. He put forward the scheme for what he called 'a Clearing House for Ideas' and persuaded Godfrey to agree to a memorandum inviting 'every member of the NID and secretarial staff (male or female) to take a hand in solving naval problems'. The best way to destroy the *Tirpitz* was one theme which produced a strong response and some good ideas.

After the German invasion of Crete Fleming began to take an interest in the activities of Otto Skorzeny and his paratroopers in that island and decided that this was something which could usefully be copied by the Royal Navy. Much later he said that it was Otto Skorzeny who inspired him to create the character of Hugo Drax in *Moonraker*.

In the words of Admiral Godfrey:

I could not have wished for a more agreeable companion than Ian Fleming on our many expeditions. I have never known him anything but buoyant, responsive and light-hearted, especially when things were going badly.

He learned more quickly than some of his R.N.V.R. colleagues that the N.I.D. was not a debating society, that orders must be obeyed promptly and not treated as a basis for discussion. He was reticent about his own affairs and kept his friends in watertight compartments, sometimes with perplexing results. He had periods of sadness and could withdraw within himself in a way that some found baffling and disconcerting.

Ian was a war winner and the country and the Navy owe a great debt to those who recommended him. I once said that Ian should have been D.N.I. and I his naval adviser.[9]

There is no doubt that one of the reasons why Fleming's services were sought by Admiral Godfrey in those summer months preceding the advent of war in 1939 was that Fleming had taken so keen an interest in obtaining information about Admiral Canaris. For, in early July 1939, Canaris sent emissaries to London to make certain inquiries on his own behalf. It was then clear that Canaris was afraid of losing contact with the potential enemy, Britain, of whom he wished to make an ally. One of Canaris's agents, Lt-Colonel Count von Schwirin, was received by Godfrey and lunched with him on 3 July.

Nothing came of this approach, and it is clear that Godfrey received no backing higher up for pursuing plans for a secret understanding with Canaris. Later, Godfrey felt sufficiently confident of his PA's competence in handling foreign naval officers who were dubious allies to send him over to France when the French capitulated in 1940. When Fleming reached France, 'he acquired a wireless set and operator by some process, the nature of which I never understood,' stated Godfrey, adding that Fleming 'was able to communicate by teleprinter at intervals en route'.[10]

The big question, of course, was to find out exactly on whose side Admiral Darlan, French Minister of Marine, really was, and whether he might be won over as a secret ally. Fleming's view was that a big mistake had been made by the British for failing to ensure that, in the event of the French Army capitulating, communications with the French Admiralty by secret cipher would be feasible. Afterwards he firmly believed that, if such communication had existed, the tragedy of the bombardment of French ships by the British at Oran could have been avoided.

Both Churchill and the Admiralty were worried about Darlan and feared he had prejudices against the British. Churchill recalled how a year previously at an Admiralty banquet Darlan had replied to a toast by reminding his hosts that his own great-grandfather had been killed at Trafalgar. Darlan had after the fall of France removed his headquarters to the Château d'Artigny, near Tours. Fleming's suggestion was that he should go immediately to the château and stay as close to Darlan as he could until the latter had made his intentions clear. Having received permission to do so, Fleming together with an air attaché from the British Embassy, made his way by road to the château. Two days later he received Darlan's message: in effect it said that Darlan appreciated the offer of safe harbour by the British, but declined it for the time being, while indicating that the war would go on as before. It was a somewhat vague message, but Darlan did at least say that two battleships, the *Richelieu* and the *Jean Bart* 'will go to England if the risk from the air is too serious or if anything really grave occurs'.

This seemed to show that Darlan still had hopes of continuing the war in some way or other. Maybe he was bluffing, or perhaps he was playing for time, but there is no doubt that the Admiralty should have shown a little more patience at this time.

Fleming wanted to stay close to Darlan and follow up developments. The Admiralty told him he must do what he could to help Britons who were being evacuated from Bordeaux. He was also told to ensure that a number of aero engines and spare parts for them should not fall into enemy hands. This work he set about with vigour and determination, even managing to persuade the captains of various neutral vessels in the estuary by Point Verdon to help in evacuating the refugees. Among the latter was King Zog of Albania, his family and crown jewels. Having seen the royal party safely aboard, Fleming pondered on the number of

Rolls-Royces and Bentleys that had to be left behind by the refugees. 'I always wondered about what the Germans thought when they came upon not only King Zog's imperial motor car, but all those Rolls-Royces and Bentleys.' Fleming commented.[11]

The most nagging problem that faced British Naval Intelligence towards the end of the summer of 1940 was that naval messages of the German Enigma signals were still not being decoded. This was a problem that Fleming was determined to try to solve personally. He worked out a quite sensational plan, which he outlined in the following memorandum to his chief, Admiral Godfrey, on 12 September 1940:

> I suggest we obtain the loot [meaning the code secrets] by the following means:
>     1   Obtain from Air Ministry an airworthy German bomber.
>     2   Pick a tough crew of five, including a pilot, W/T operator and word-perfect German speaker. Dress them in German Air Force uniforms, add blood and bandages to suit.
>     3   Crash plane in the Channel after making S.O.S. to rescue service in P/L [plain language].
>     4   Once aboard rescue boat, shoot German crew, dump overboard, bring rescue boat back to English port.
>     'In order to increase the chances of capturing an R. or M. [*Räumboot* = small minesweeper; *Minensuchboot* = large minesweeper] with its richer booty, the crash might be staged in mid-Channel. The Germans would presumably employ one of this type for the longer and more hazardous journey.[12]

Fleming received support for this adventurous project and, as a result, set to work on a further development of his scheme. The aim was of course to obtain the German code secrets from the captured minesweeper, and the proposed undercover mission was given the code-name Operation Ruthless. Fleming thought the best plan would be to carry out the operation shortly before dawn with a twin-engine Heinkel which he had managed to obtain from the Air Ministry. This aircraft had crash-landed in Scotland during a raid on the Firth of Forth and had not been severely damaged.

One factor in favour of the plan was that no British naval secrets or codes would be given away if it failed.

Adding more details to the project, Fleming insisted that when the aircraft headed across the Channel, a close watch should be kept for the appearance of a German minesweeper and, when one was spotted, the Heinkel should cut an engine, pour out smoke and drop into the water. When the British, dressed in German uniform, were 'rescued' by the crew of the German minesweeper, they were to shoot to kill, take charge of the ship and sail it back to England.

Apparently those in the RAF responsible for evaluating captured German aircraft took a somewhat critical view of Operation Ruthless. Nevertheless they agreed to co-operate and Fleming personally went down to the Channel coast to supervise preparations. Several days passed by and reports from the Air Ministry were that they had not been able to spot any suitable German vessel operating at night in the chosen area. On 16 October it was decided to switch the operation to the Portsmouth area instead. Yet for some reason or other no satisfactory reports came in to enable the operation to be launched. Fleming was bitterly disappointed and urged that the watch for a suitable German ship should be stepped up and that the help of the Secret Service and others be sought in getting the right answers. Incredibly, even in November 1940, there was no satisfactory response and so this audacious enterprise was never attempted. Yet at Bletchley, where the main deciphering work was done, there was outrage at the apparent failure of the Air Ministry or others to spot even a small German minesweeper after so long a wait. All the top boffins at Bletchley were enthusiastic about the scheme: indeed, some of them saw it as the only hope for speedily breaking Enigma.

# 4

# *Launching the OSS*

Referring to the visit of Admiral Godfrey and Fleming to
Washington in 1941, Patrick Beesly of the NID wrote:
'Fleming drafted plans which led to the creation of the
O.S.S.'[1]

O ne of the problems facing the NID in the early months of
1941 was relations with the ONI, the American Office of
Naval Intelligence. Following the First World War the ONI had
diminished from a wartime maximum of 306 officers and eighteen
clerks to eighteen officers and a handful of civilians. Rear-
Admiral A.F. Niblack, who was then Director of the ONI, had
not been keen on espionage and wanted to 'get back to the
old-fashioned system with a naval attaché who is a member of the
diplomatic corps and who conforms to all the conventionalities'.[2]

As the war in Europe developed, views began to change. In
January 1941 a Special Activities Branch of the ONI was set up
under Commander J.L. Riheldaffer, USN. This change of attitude
was partly due to the fact that Naval Intelligence in the United
States had played a part in solving four cases of espionage between 1936 and 1940. Relations on intelligence matters between
the US Army and Navy were not always satisfactory and there was
the added complication for the ONI not only of working along
with Army Intelligence, but with the FBI and Customs and Im-
migration officials in clearance and interrogation operations with
PanAm Clipper aircraft and merchant ships from Europe. To
make matters worse, there was no joint intelligence machinery in
Washington and the result was that, rather than co-operating properly, the departments of intelligence liked scooping each other.

Then in August 1940 Colonel William (later General) Donovan, a New York lawyer, who frequently conducted intelligence
inquiries at his own expense, went to London to try to find out the
truth about British intentions: would Britain fight on at all costs,
or, as the defeatist Ambassador Joseph Kennedy kept reporting
back to Washington, ultimately give in? Donovan's visit was welcomed both by Cordell Hull, the Secretary of State, and Frank
Knox, the Navy Secretary. Donovan met Admiral Godfrey and
had a long talk with him. They took an instant liking to each other
and from then on Godfrey decided that Donovan was the man
from whom to seek help – 'much more so,' said Fleming afterwards, 'than anyone in the ONI'.

Meanwhile Fleming decided that priority should be given to two
things: first, making friends with Americans generally and learn-
ing to appreciate their viewpoints more considerately; and,
second, to improve relations with the ONI. That he succeeded is
perhaps best illustrated by the comment of Admiral Godfrey that
'Ian got on well with Americans: operating on a slightly different
plane to mine, he was able to discover how the land lay and to
warn me of pitfalls. He ensured that everything I wrote was to the
point, devoid of ambiguity and worded in a way that appealed to
the Americans.'[3]

One way in which Fleming paved the way to better relations
with the Americans was by his unofficial revelations to them of
rather more of the truth behind the Tyler Kent case than they
would otherwise have acquired. He was able to stress that not
only was Kent, a member of the US Embassy staff who was
arrested by the British for espionage in 1940, apparently responsible for passing information to the Germans, but to the USSR
as well. Fleming was able to point out to his American contacts
that Tyler Kent had been closely associated in London with
known Soviet agents. Tyler Kent had of course previously served
in the US Embassy in Moscow. Fleming himself had learned that
while MI5 had identified Kent as a security risk eight months
before they had tipped off the US Embassy, he took the view that
this was a bad example of how to conduct relations with the
Americans. That he was justified can perhaps best be appreciated
by the comment of Herschal V. Johnson, the US Counsellor, that

'it was most regrettable that Scotland Yard had not informed us of these circumstances at the time. We would never have left the man in the code room if there had been the slightest suspicion against him'.

Fleming also went out of his way to remind Americans of the brilliance of the celebrated Admiral 'Blinker' Hall, who was DNI in the 1914–18 war. He was still somewhat of a legend to the Americans because of his feat in deciphering the notorious Zimmerman Telegram in which the Germans proposed to make an ally of Mexico in return for which they would support Mexico's claims to recover such territories of the United States as Texas, New Mexico and Arizona. All this helped to pave the way for the visit to the United States of Godfrey and Fleming in May 1941. The proposal for the visit came from the American Naval Intelligence through Colonel (later Major-General Sir Robert) Neville, Royal Marines, who was Assistant Director of Naval Intelligence at the Admiralty. When this news came through, Fleming strongly urged Godfrey to make sure that on his visit he made direct contacts with all branches of American Intelligence and not the ONI alone.

'It was Ian Fleming who accompanied me to Washington and New York in the summer of 1941. We flew in the Clipper via Bermuda and one of our passengers was Schiaparelli on her way to start a *haute couture* establishment in New York. Bermuda is renowned for its underwater flora and fauna so I took the precaution of including a pair of underwater goggles in my luggage.'[4]

Godfrey and Fleming were both somewhat concerned when they arrived in the United States about the large number of press photographers at the airport. They feared their visit would no longer be kept secret. However, they were much relieved when they saw that the photographers' target was not themselves but Schiaparelli. The primary aim of this mission was of course to ensure, despite the fact that the United States was still neutral, that there was complete co-operation between the NID and the ONI. It is clear that Godfrey used Fleming for the more informal and adventurous approaches on this subject. Fleming initiated the idea of eventually achieving such co-operation in London as well as in Washington. Eventually he succeeded in this by having an ONI officer attached to him in London, namely Lt Alan Schneider, who was stationed at the US Naval Headquarters in 18 Grosvenor Square, just across the way from the US Embassy.

At the same time Fleming, still insistent on keeping in touch with all sections of American Intelligence, was turning his attention to Colonel Donovan, whom he regarded not only as one of the best allies Britain could have across the Atlantic, but potentially the ideal man for the very job which at that time the United States lacked – the chief of Secret Service. In trying to bring this about Fleming won the support of William Stephenson, the Canadian who had been chosen to take charge of British Intelligence in the United States. Fleming was fortunate in that Stephenson and Donovan were friends and knew each other respectively as 'Little Bill' and 'Big Bill'. Meanwhile Godfrey had something of a shock when he had an interview with President Roosevelt. The latter spoke to Godfrey of his great admiration for 'Blinker' Hall, whom he had come to know when he was Under-Secretary of the Navy in the First World War. 'Of course he had a wonderful intelligence service,' said Roosevelt, 'but I don't suppose it's much good now!'[5]

'We've got to be careful', Fleming told Godfrey, 'that we are not accused of trying to put "Big Bill" under "Little Bill's" control. This is a hand we have got to play very carefully, or we are in danger of being trumped. However, we've already won one hand. Donovan has smoothed over a number of our problems with the ONI.'

Cautiously working behind the scenes, secretly seeing Stephenson and some of his agents, keeping in touch with Donovan and urging that the Americans should have something like the Joint Intelligence Committee and Staff modelled on Britain's JIC, Fleming made progress. His ambition was not merely to see Donovan given real powers as an Intelligence chief, but to pave the way for the setting up of a new American Secret Service. With this in mind Fleming had drafted for Donovan a memorandum that set out his ideas of what exactly this new Secret Service should consist. It was a bold and determined move, and in some ways almost outrageous. However, Fleming managed to word the memorandum in tactful language. For example, it started off as follows: 'In accordance with your request, the following sugges-tions concerned with the obtaining of intelligence through United States sources and the cooperation of U.S. Intelligence Services with our own are submitted privately.'

The note went on to say that 'Admiral Godfrey, D.N.I., has seen these suggestions and concurs generally in them. A copy of this memorandum will also be shown to Admiral Danckwerts. It is requested that no action may be taken on any of these suggestions referring to the S.I.S. [UK Secret Intelligence Service] without prior consultation with Mr Stephenson or without the full concur-rence of his chief [in this case, Colonel Stewart Menzies]'.

What Fleming went on to urge was that the State Department should send a circular telegram to all their diplomatic and consu-lar posts in Axis or Axis-occupied territory, requesting certain specific information.[6] Fleming had an original approach to intelligence-gathering. He wished to allow for the collection of the unexpected, the chance remark that would provide the vital clue to some unsolved riddle. He wanted the people collecting intelli-gence not to be afraid of submitting some ideas and comments of their own. Donovan commented afterwards that 'Ian's idea of giving the individual scope for thinking for himself was splendid, but sometimes it resulted in our getting a whole lot of nonsense which wasted our time. Donovan, then middle-aged, had served with the US forces in the First World War and had ever since taken an interest in military matters and especially in strategy. He deplored the fact that the United States had no secret service. He was a remarkable character in every way: a Southerner, a Catholic and a Republican, yet on the very best terms with the Democratic President Roosevelt. He was well aware of the feelings of some politicians and even Service officers that there was something disreputable and 'un-American' about espionage. He was suf-ficiently tactful to allow for such sentiments when putting forward his ideas. Fleming's proposals helped him in this respect, as they steered cautiously clear of anything smacking of the more out-rageous elements of intelligence-gathering.

Fleming suggested to Donovan that American intelligence-gatherers in the proposed new organization should eventually be given training by British agents. This proposal was supported by Stephenson, who had already set up his own training centre in Canada, the mysterious 'Camp X'. Nevertheless it was some time before it became clear whether the plan for setting up an United States Secret Service would succeed. Donovan had further talks with the President and he submitted to Roosevelt a detailed memorandum which included several of Fleming's ideas. This was dated 10 June 1941, and in it Donovan urged the creation of a 'Service of Strategic Information'.[7] A number of military officers of high rank opposed the plan, but in the following month a presidential order was made and the OSS (Office of Strategic Services) was established, with Donovan as its chief.

There were some politicians and Service officers who thought that the new service should come under the FBI (Federal Bureau of Investigation). Fleming, who had no great regard for Edgar Hoover, chief of the FBI, had hinted either in his own memorandum or verbally that, while there should be links with the FBI, the new organization should be independent of it. Within three weeks of his talk with the President, Donovan had been given a budget of some $3 million to develop the OSS. In return for the help and encouragement he had had from Fleming he assisted decisively in smoothing out difficulties in the relationship between the NID and ONI.

Fleming took full advantage on his various visits to the United States of building up his relationship with Stephenson, whose code-name was Intrepid, which he continued to use as his telegraphic address in Bermuda after he retired. Stephenson was of course the prime link between his undercover intelligence set-up in New York and Stewart Menzies and MI6 in London. After serving in the Royal Flying Corps in the First World War Stephenson had become a pioneer in broadcasting and the radio transmission of photographs as well as being involved in a film company in London and the manufacture of plastics and the steel industry. He had also won the King's Cup air race in 1934 with a machine that had been built in one of his factories. Fleming had a great admiration for Stephenson, whom he later described as 'one of the great secret agents of the last war' in a foreword he wrote to the American edition of a biography of Stephenson. It is probable that Fleming's mistrust of Edgar Hoover was to some extent the result of Stephenson's own constant problems in dealing with the FBI. Nevertheless, despite being loyal to his friend's memory, Fleming later came to have considerable doubts about some of Stephenson's claims, though he never expressed them in print. Since his death Stephenson has been accused of making a number of fraudulent claims, even to the extent of producing a forged letter from Winston Churchill which was reproduced in the book *A Man Called Intrepid*. Sir John Colville, Churchill's private secretary, called the letter 'a clear invention', if only because 'for obvious reasons' Churchill never signed himself 'WC'.[8]

Stephenson and Fleming had had a lengthy talk in New York prior to the latter's meeting with Donovan and the presentation of his memorandum. This was at the Rockefeller Center, from which Stephenson operated the organization he called British Security Coordination. It was through this organization that Stephenson kept links with both the SIS and SOE (Special Operations Executive). There have of course been attempts by some to minimize the influence of Fleming's memorandum on Donovan. Thomas Troy, the historian of the CIA, has described some of Fleming's recommendations as being 'commonplace or unrealistic'.[9] 'Fleming was hardly Donovan's ghostwriter,' declared Richard Dunlop, Donovan's biographer, in referring to Donovan's *Memorandum on the Establishment of a Service of Strategic Information*. But neither Fleming, nor anyone on the British side, made any such suggestion.

Ivar Bryce, who should know something about this whole affair, has stated that Fleming 'had been whisked off to a room in the new annexe of the Embassy, locked in it with a pen and paper and the necessities of life, and had written, under armed guard around the clock, a document of some seventy pages covering every aspect of a giant secret intelligence and secret operational organization'.[10] Seventy pages! One would like to have seen every word of this document, as doubtless it would have included many touches of Flemingesque phraseology which the summary already mentioned did not include. One such item was the piece of advice he gave Donovan to 'make an example of someone at an early date for indiscretion, and continue to act ruthlessly where lack of security is concerned'.[11]

That Donovan greatly appreciated Fleming's advice and suggestions is clear from the fact that long afterwards he presented the PA to the DNI with a .38 Colt revolver inscribed 'For Special Services'. It was a souvenir of which Fleming was very proud.

As already noted, one of Stephenson's creations was Camp X, an SOE training school for secret agents on the Canadian shore of Lake Ontario. Not only did they get special training in the arts of combat and undercover activities, but Hollywood artists created special disguises for them. The whole Camp X story remains to this day something of a mixture of myth and reality, with many of the myths predominating. No doubt Stephenson's talent for embellishing the truth played a part in all this.

Some of these myths touch upon the subject of Fleming and his visit to Camp X. In John Pearson's biography of Fleming the author says that Ian 'suggested that he spent a few days there [at Camp X] as a trainee. It was to prove a formidable experience'.[12] The question arises, at what date did Fleming make this visit? Camp X did not come into existence before late 1941 or early 1942 and it was closed down early in 1944, so any such trip must have been in 1942 or 1943. If he went to Camp X, it might have been through the influence either of Stephenson or of his friend Ivar Bryce, who worked for the SOE in New York as well as helping to recruit agents to work for the British in Latin America.

The story goes that Fleming took the self-defence and unarmed combat courses and that he received top marks for the underwater exercise. This involved an underwater swim by night to an old tanker moored offshore in the lake. His set task was to fix a limpet mine to the hull of the vessel. As Dr David Stafford, an authority on Camp X, writes:

> It was remarkably like James Bond's later performance against
> Mr Big in *Live and Let Die*. . . . Like his fictional hero,
> Fleming succeeded in putting the mine in place and then
> escaping undetected. Another of his outstanding achievements
> was in the 'Agents Initiative' test. Here, trainees had to place
> an imaginary bomb in the main Toronto power station. Their
> task was made more difficult because the station was heavily
> guarded and because the city police had been deliberately

alerted. Those who tried to sneak past the guards in disguise were caught. Fleming alone succeeded. He did so by using the best disguise of all: himself. He telephoned the plant manager, explained in his best English accent and Old Etonian manner that he was a visiting expert from Britain, arranged a formal tour, and was ushered through the gates by welcoming guards.[13]

Nevertheless Dr Stafford, who has made a detailed study of this Canadian school for secret agents, is doubtful about some of the stories told about Fleming in Camp X. Fleming may well have visited the place, but it seems doubtful that he stayed there long. In any case, would he have had the time to spare for a lengthy training course in view of the constant pressure of his other work? Dr Stafford says that neither Bill Brooker nor Cuthbert Skilbeck, the two living commandants of Camp X, has any recollection of Fleming's having been there. Yet Stephenson says that Fleming was one of the school's best pupils and the only one to succeed in the Agent's Initiative test!

Alan Schneider tells a somewhat different story. This ONI officer, later to be attached to Fleming, went to an agents' training school in the United Kingdom where he met instructors who had been at Camp X.

When they found out that I was Ian's opposite number they told me about his progress at the school. He had done very well with the various small arms and seemed to like the sub-machine-gun particularly. . . . In the exercises requiring intelligence and imagination he was one of the best. . . . I am sure a lot of this school went into his books. . . . However, in spite of all this, the opinion was unanimous that he would not have made a satisfactory agent in the field. The trouble, they said, was that although Ian was an outstanding trainee, he just did not have the temperament for an agent in the field. . . . It was not that he lacked courage – he had a great deal of that. But, they said, he had far too much imagination.[14]

The story is that the final test for the trainees at Camp X was designed to find out if they had the nerve to kill. A room would be booked at an hotel in Toronto, the trainee would be given its

name and the number of the room and told that a dangerous
enemy agent located there had to be eliminated. Fleming is supposed to have been sent there with a loaded gun on just such a
message. Apparently the man in this room was a highly skilled
instructor who knew exactly how to divert his attacker sufficiently
for the bullet to miss him. Fleming, so Alan Schneider and others
were told, went up to the door of the room and then turned away,
explaining afterwards that he couldn't kill a man in cold blood.

The story itself is highly improbable. If some heedless instructors designed such a test, it is likely that Fleming showed it up for
the nonsense it was. Alan Schneider's comment is particularly
interesting: 'I never mentioned this to Ian and, actually, just
hearing about it upset me. The only motives I could ascribe to the
man telling me about it were not good ones. A lot of British
officers I met made snide and sometimes sarcastic remarks about
him. I always felt, and still do, that they were jealous and
envious.'[15]

Dr Stafford can find no trace of a 'Colonel Wallace', one of the
instructors mentioned in the Camp X–Fleming stories, ever having been at the training station. If he had been there at any time,
he must have used a cover name. 'Fleming was a celebrity and
celebrities were good for the story of B.S.C. [British Security
Coordination] and its various activities. . . . Camp X validates
Fleming's claim to direct expertise in the creation of James Bond
himself, and also a central part of the Camp X story as it is
constantly retailed by word of mouth and popular histories. . . .
Camp X has become a cipher for grandiose fantasies about spy-
masters and secret agents in the Second World War.'[16]

It is more than likely that the fantasist Stephenson was the
source of at least some of these stories. He claimed to have been
awarded the *Légion d'honneur* by the French, but there is no
record of it. Similarly there is no confirmation of his other claim
that he had been 'amateur lightweight world champion' at boxing.

Another story about Fleming that has been somewhat embel-
lished in the telling was the incident on which he partly based the
casino gambling scene in *Casino Royale*. When he and Admiral
Godfrey stopped off at Lisbon *en route* for the United States,
Fleming decided to try his luck at the tables. During the play he

whispered to Godfrey that if two chaps playing were German agents, as he suspected, it would be a splendid plan to take them on and remove all their cash. Godfrey was dubious of the wisdom of such a ploy, but, so the tale goes, Fleming played on, failed to win and was eventually cleaned out of his cash.

Dusko Popov, the double agent code-named 'Tricycle', who was also in Lisbon during Fleming's visit there, tells a somewhat different story of the incident. Popov was one of the agents used by the British in their 'Double Cross' game: he was used to exploit the Germans while posing as one of their agents. He had just been given $80,000 by the Germans for services rendered and this sum he was going to hand over to the British the following morning. Having met Fleming in the hotel where he was staying before dinner, he felt certain that the former knew all about this money.

In his book *Spy-Counter-Spy*, Popov wrote:

> British Intelligence had enough confidence to entrust me with 80,000 dollars. The secrets I carried in my head were worth much more. We strolled through the halls of the casino, my shadow and I, observing play at different tables. A favourite *bête noire* of mine was there – an insignificant but wealthy Lithuanian named Bloch, who attempted to compensate for his tiny stature by arrogant play. . . . I don't know what the devil was behind me, perhaps Fleming or the knowledge that he was there, but when Bloch announced *'Banque ouverte'*, I announced 'Fifty thousand dollars.' I glanced at Fleming. His face turned bile green. Obviously the Lithuanian didn't have that sort of money on him. He squirmed in his chair in embarrassment.[17]

Eventually the bet was not taken, thus enabling Fleming to recover his nerve. That is Popov's version of the affair. The detailed story of gambling at the tables in *Casino Royale* certainly suggested that Fleming had a thorough knowledge of casino gambling practices and jargon. However, I learned from Stephen Coulter, who later was Fleming's chosen correspondent in Paris, that it was he who, at Fleming's request, supplied the background information on this subject which was used in the book.

Donald McLachlan, who is a particularly reliable witness, has this version of the Lisbon incident. He told how Godfrey and Fleming met members of the British Embassy, who told them of the goings-on among German secret agents in Lisbon.

> When Fleming heard that the German Intelligence chiefs gambled every night in the casino at Estoril, he suggested that the D.N.I. and himself should go and join them at the *chemin de fer*. The Admiral did not know the game so Fleming decided to sit it out himself and gamble against these men – in the hope, as he put it, of reducing German secret service funds. With only £50 in travelling money, he was quickly defeated and cleaned out. The D.N.I. was not impressed, but this was how the whole Bond business started.[18]

There is no doubt that Fleming's memorandum enabled Donovan to put his case to the President much more effectively than would otherwise have been possible. As Donovan confided to colleagues later: 'I was given a far better picture of what a secret service can achieve by being shown what the British N.I.D. were actually doing than anything I had been told elsewhere.'

Fleming had taken great care in his memorandum not to overstate his case and, even more important, to be very cautious in recommending the type of person who should be employed in the proposed US Secret Service. Fleming's view was that any suggestion of unorthodox characters – 'men of the Sidney Reilly school of espionage', as he dubbed them – would offend the somewhat old-maidish brigade among the older American politicians and servicemen who still regarded espionage as a dirty game.

In his history of the OSS Richard Harris Smith refers to Fleming's having recommended that officers for the new service should be 'about forty to fifty. Donovan declined Fleming's advice. Instead he promised Franklin Roosevelt an international secret service staffed by young officers who were "calculatingly reckless" with "disciplined daring" and "trained for aggressive action."'[19]

The curious feature of all this is, of course, that what Donovan urged on Roosevelt sounds much more like Fleming's real self than the cautious advice in his memorandum. Those quoted phrases from Donovan's memorandum to Roosevelt are very much Fleming's style of expression, especially 'calculatingly reckless'. It is more than likely that Fleming followed up his written work by giving Donovan a verbal off-the-cuff suggestion of just how much further he might experiment in choosing personnel.

# 5

## *The Luring of Rudolf Hess*

The significance of Hitler's belief in horoscopy and of
astrological data given to Hitler, being the same as that
evolved by any sincere astrologer in this country, was
discussed [in 1940]. Our astrologers foretold that Hitler's star
would begin to wane in the New Year.[1]

M uch of the information in this chapter is so far removed
from reality, so totally bizarre in many of its aspects, that it
presents traps at every turning for a biographer. It is largely to
give the chapter some kind of authority and credence that I have
put the quotation from Admiral Godfrey as a starting-point. It
seems essential that the puzzled reader should know at once that
astrology, the occult and many other fantastic cults were actually
studied and employed during the war by the NID.

To underline the significance of this it is necessary to give the
full text of Godfrey's comments on the subject. 'Our astrologers',
as he called them, had told him that all Hitler wanted to achieve
'must be done by the end of February 1941. All that has not been
done yet will have to be done now quickly, and it may include
another peaceful arrangement which, however, had little chance
of success. After March 1941, Hitler's luck will be out'.[2]

Godfrey went on to say:

Hitler's invasion of Russia took place when Hitler's astrological
'aspects' were at their shakiest. An unknown commentator has
referred to my flirtation with astrology as 'NID at its most
unexpected'. It may seem odd and some may think it a waste of
time that we should have turned aside from straight intelligence
even for a moment into the realms of necromancy. . . . If one's

opponent is known to be a man who places faith in horoscopy
and if, as we are assured, it is an exact science, based on the
date, time and place of birth, it would surely be unwise to
neglect the existence of any advice being tendered to him if, as
we believed, our own people knew who were giving the advice
and could say what it was.[3]

To what extent Fleming encouraged such attention to the occult
and horoscope casters is a matter of conjecture. One can picture
him rather cleverly supporting such ploys with mild cynicism, but
adding: 'If it supplies some clues, we shall gain where more
orthodox Intelligence Services lose out.' The important point to
remember is that the mysterious Vanessa had first aroused his
interest in such matters and that, as he discovered the extent to
which the Nazis and Hess in particular took astrology seriously, so
he became an enthusiastic advocate of taking advantage of this.

Vanessa Hoffmann had arranged to communicate with Fleming
through a character who used the curious alibi of 'Bill Findearth'
and who had contacts with the anti-fascist intelligence network in
Switzerland, which became known as PAKBO. 'Findearth's
mother was English and he himself was a Finn,' I was told. 'On
the Continent he used the name of "Werther".' A man with the
code-name of 'Findearth' was one of the unofficial contacts of Sir
Basil Thomson when he organized the Special Branch at Scotland
Yard after the First World War and he was devoted to combating
the early menace of Soviet espionage in Britain. His papers, made
available to me some years ago, mention Findearth as 'a lively and
accurate informant on Soviet activities in Finland as they affect
the United Kingdom'. Long after I had seen these papers, further
information coming through to me suggested that Findearth was
much more important than I had at first realized.

During the Second World War, while I was in New York, I had
been introduced to a character who called himself William van
Narvig by Wythe Williams, who was then editor of a small
suburban newspaper called *Greenwich Time* which had frequently
produced some startling world scoops, especially on what was
going on in Germany and Soviet Russia. The man behind these
scoops was none other than William van Narvig. As time went on

I became fascinated with the character of van Narvig who, it seemed to me, must be the super-spy of all time, a man who had shown he was able equally to infiltrate both the Kremlin and the Gestapo. He had produced for *Greenwich Time* such astonishing scoops as the Hitler-Stalin Pact, the German invasion of Denmark and France and later the threat to the Western world of the Soviet Union. For a long time, however, I began to think that he could not be a real person and that somehow he had been invented by Wythe Williams as a cover-up for the real source of his scoops. Eventually, I obtained copies of FBI official papers on this extraordinary character and I discovered that his real name was William Otto Lucas, born in St Petersburg, and that he had become an American citizen.[4]

Eventually I wrote a book about this remarkable man who, even during the Second World War, managed to travel both in Germany and the USSR.[5] But this book's publication was delayed for many years because Lucas disappeared completely around 1954 and, though I tried hard to trace him and his family, nothing new turned up. Meanwhile Fleming had confirmed to me that he had known this man by the name of Findearth. 'Only Naval Intelligence would give him any credence over here, I'm afraid' was Fleming's comment. 'His mother had known my mother's family and I was given an introduction to him by a German girl I met in Switzerland. But I couldn't tell you where he is now.'

I rather doubted this latter statement at the time, but I am sure Fleming was telling the truth, as all my efforts to advertise in American papers and periodicals for information on Lucas and his family failed to produce results.

I am merely making an intelligent guess that Vanessa was the girl who introduced Ian to Findearth, or Lucas. But the information which this mysterious character provided tends to support this view, for it was Lucas who, having failed to get another branch of Britain's Secret Service to concern itself in the Nazis' interest in astrology and the occult, managed to get his intelligence-gathering accepted by Naval Intelligence. For by this time he had built up his own contacts of moles inside the Gestapo. The vital information was that Hitler's deputy leader, Rudolf Hess, was not only keenly interested in astrological forecasts but had grave doubts about carrying on a war against the British: he regarded the Soviet Union as Germany's only real enemy.

'Nobody else would listen about Hess and astrology,' Fleming told me. 'Even our people were doubtful, but I kept pushing them. In the end it was suggested that NID couldn't do much, but someone else might, and I decided to be the someone else who might effectively exploit this idea.' Fleming asked me not to breathe a word of this story while he was alive – 'if you live that long,' he added smilingly with his inevitable brand of black humour.

'Fleming had studied the dossier on Admiral Sir Barry Domville, the pro-German Director of Naval Intelligence in the period of 1927–30, and this had led him to examine, first of all out of idle curiosity, the history of The Link [the Anglo-German society that came into existence after Hitler's coming to power]. He had also had a keen insight into the psychological make-up of the German character and of the preoccupation of top-ranking Nazis with astrology and the occult. Consequently he thought up the idea of re-creating The Link during wartime and building up a fictitious picture of how it had gone underground and acquired new and even more influential members who could pave the way to a negotiated peace with Germany and the overthrow of the Churchill government. If this kind of information could be leaked to some gullible Nazi leader, he believed that not only might Germany's invasion plans be shelved but that Nazis could be misled into secretly sending some important figure in their hierarchy to Britain.'[6]

Fleming was unquestionably influenced by the views of his brother Peter, who firmly believed that if Hitler had put three or four divisions across the English Channel immediately after Dunkirk, he might well have succeeded in making a successful invasion of Britain. The need to forestall any later attempt by the Nazis to invade was therefore of paramount importance. In 1940–1 it was essential to hoodwink the Nazis into believing that a peace deal with Britain could be achieved, thus delaying invasion in the meantime. It was a dangerous game, but it was one of the very few cards Britain had left to play. Fleming knew only too well what a hazardous game this could be and how it could go against the

Government's policy, and this was one reason why to a large extent he played it on his own, independently of the NID at times and using other contacts. Churchill's policy was quite the reverse: he did not wish to disguise the prospect of invasion from the British people, but to convince them that they were in danger of it. He knew perfectly well that there was no imminent prospect of invasion at that time, but evidently his policy was to prolong the war, not to halt it. So that the British people should not be lulled into believing that peace terms could be made with Germany, he deliberately provoked the bombing of London. There is today every indication from German records that Hitler had forbidden the bombing of British cities such as London. It was for this reason that Churchill forced Hitler's hand and started to bomb Berlin, despite the fact that he was warned by Sir Charles Portal, at that time commander-in-chief of Bomber Command, that this might lead to the Germans lifting their embargo on the bombing of London.

Feeling that speed of action was needed, Fleming decided to bypass his own NID and push his project in other quarters. He felt it was too hazardous to handle on his own, but, reluctant to let go of a scheme that appealed to his imaginative mind, he passed the idea on to two trusted friends, one who was in another branch of British Intelligence and the other a contact in Switzerland who was an authority in astrology. Throughout these negotiations William Otto Lucas was a key figure. As far as I can gather this was very much a private operation of Fleming's, which to some extent Godfrey tolerated, and it had nothing, officially at least, to do with MI6.

Briefly, Fleming's plan had three aims: the first was to convince Germans that The Link had been revived and that there was still a powerful peace party in Britain; the second was to manipulate Hess by feeding him with bogus astrological predictions; and the third was to link up with other occultists who claimed to have useful German connections. However, as such ploys are liable to be misunderstood, it should be stressed that Fleming genuinely saw such tactics as being essential if Britain were to be safeguarded from invasion. In other words, to play for time until Britain was able to cope with the enemy.

Fleming's three aims involved him in a great deal of work outside his NID activities. Stories concocted about the revival of The Link had to be planted overseas and passed on through agents in the Café Chiada in Lisbon and another café in Berne. Fleming's methods of work on such occasions were frequently circumlocutory and, where and when he saw fit, deliberately obscure. He had the uncanny skill when briefing people of giving less than the information required, thus disguising the purpose of an operation while cajoling some mystified subordinate into doing the right thing while keeping him in the dark about the object of the exercise. All this time Fleming was encouraged by the intelligence he was receiving privately and outside the ranks of the NID on the possibility of establishing an understanding with Admiral Canaris. It was Canaris much more than Hess whom Fleming would have liked to lure to Britain.

Hess, however, presented a somewhat easier target. Vanessa Hoffmann's information convinced him that while Canaris could not be won over by any faked horoscopes, Hess might well be exploited in this way. Fortunately, through the help of Vanessa Hoffmann, detailed information about Hess, his ideas and habits, was provided by a young secretary named Helga Stultz, who was working in the archives of the Berghof and who became an informant to US Intelligence later in the war. She passed on details of Hess's private intelligence service and the astonishing news that 'Hess sides with Hitler; he believes that Germany must settle her account with Russia and that by doing so some agreement can be reached with England. . . . Hess is contemptuous of the *Abwehr* and is pursuing his own ideas of espionage.' This report, so Fleming discovered later, was passed on to Washington.

It is now clear that one of Fleming's most brilliant ideas was to tap the information pouring into Wythe Williams's newspaper, *Greenwich Time*. Not all of this information was published in *Greenwich Time*: Wythe Williams was strongly pro-British and kept back anything which he felt might be unhelpful to the war effort. Then came this vital message:

Last night Hess had a long talk with Hitler in the latter's study. Hess returned from a trip to Madrid only a few days ago. He travelled incognito and no one had the faintest idea of what it all meant. The first clue I obtained of these doings was through Hess's talk with Hitler. Hess went to Spain on his own initiative. . . . He went to Madrid for the purpose of reaching Sir Samuel Hoare, British Ambassador. . . . While he had discussed the project with no one, not even Hitler, the Gestapo apparently had gotten wind of it. Anyway, Hess has complained to Hitler that Himmler was despatched to Madrid hurriedly so that the Gestapo chief could spy on Hess. Hess said he would have remained in Madrid if Himmler had not urged him to return to Germany. While in Madrid Hess did not see Sir Samuel Hoare, but he contrived to reach the British through friendly Spanish sources – Hess gained the impression that his suggestions might meet with consideration if he could get them to the direct attention of certain circles in England. He mentioned several names to Hitler, but he pronounced them so hurriedly that I could not get them [Helga Stultz worked in a room adjacent to Hitler's office]. Now this is what Hess proposes to do. He wants to fly to England alone. This undertaking in itself, he contends, would be so spectacular that the warmongers now directing British policy could not keep it a secret.[7]

This message was received by Fleming, almost certainly through the good offices of Vanessa Hoffmann, before it reached Wythe Williams in Greenwich, Connecticut. It was not until after the news of Hess's landing in Scotland that Williams received it. Williams felt that from a security point of view it was too risky to publish a story in his own paper, but eventually an article appeared in *Liberty Magazine*, supposedly based on a secret radio message from the tiny neutral state of Liechtenstein.[8]

There was everything to be gained and nothing to be lost by planting faked horoscopes on Hess. Fleming had discovered through various of his occultist friends such as Aleister Crowley and Ellic Howe that Hess regularly consulted astrologers and that one of these was Karl Ernest Krafft. Therefore it was essential that the horoscopes planted on Hess did not differ too markedly from those he was getting in Germany. Exactly how the bogus horoscopes were worded, or the advice they gave to Hess, remains a mystery. It is probable that Fleming himself never knew the exact phraseology given. It had to be worded in a manner that would not give Hess any cause for suspicion, but at the same time give him encouragement to make a trip to Britain. Ellic Howe's part in these activities may never be told. He never revealed anything himself, but in his book *The Black Game* (1982) he described how he was recruited into the secret services without ever being told which branch he had joined. Being tactful, he never asked! One of his tasks was to create typefaces for a fake issue of *Zenit*, a German astrological magazine. As a result, he made a lengthy study of Nazi occultism which he presented in great detail in two other books, *Nostradamus and the Nazis* (1965) and *Urania's Children* (1967).

Nicholas Campion, one of the founders of the Institute for the Study of Cycles in World Affairs and a leading astrologer, says that he

> . . . cast the horoscope for the time at which Hess took off from Germany. It was most inauspicious. It transpires that this is a most evil horoscope in any traditional sense, largely because six planets were in the house of death and two other points were strong: the fixed star Algol (which leads one to lose one's head) and the evil degree Serpentis, so called 'the accursed degree of the accursed sign'. It follows that if Hess picked the time of his flight from astrological advice, then the astrologers advising him were well aware that they were picking a time which, from the astrological point of view, predicted not only failure but death.[9]

The implication here is of course that if Hess had received orthodox astrological predictions, he would have been warned against making the trip. That he was anxious to make it appears unquestionable in the light of subsequent events, and perhaps the distorted horoscope or horoscopes which he was given enabled him to make up his mind. One of his contacts was Karl Haushofer, who knew a number of prominent British politicians and diplomats personally. In September 1940 Karl and his son Albrecht Haushofer were corresponding with Hess about ways for entering into secret negotiations with the British. When Hess received certain encouraging messages from Britain, it was suggested to him by his own intelligence service that they might be bogus and concocted by British Intelligence. From all reports he was irritated by any such suggestion. This was later confirmed by Dr Heinz Haushofer, son of Albrecht.[10]

The peace feelers from Britain to Hess were conducted largely through Lisbon and Switzerland and the former Danzig Governor Burkhardt, then head of the International Red Cross, who was in a good position to check on the various views in each country as he travelled around on his 'mercy missions'.

During this period, however, there was a much more bizarre attempt to influence Hess and others in his circle, in which Fleming was involved. The PA to the DNI had contacted Aleister Crowley, who at that time had an address in Jermyn Street: according to the late Rosa Lewis they met at the Cavendish Hotel on occasions. Fleming was convinced that there were other ways in which the Nazis could be fooled and that Crowley with his knowledge of the occult and especially of German occultism could produce the answer.

One of the British agents who had escaped from the Nazis to England was a Hungarian-born astrologer, Louis de Wohl. Largely on account of his claims to having an intimate knowledge of the methods of one of Hitler's own astrologers, he was made a captain in the British Army and attached to the Department of Psychological Warfare. In 1932 one Martin Pfefferkorn had founded a Nazi Astrologers' Study Group (*Arbeitsgemeinschaft Deutscher Astrologen*) and by the time the Nazis came to power quite a number of them had begun to pay attention to astrology, Goebbels even establishing in his ministry a department of occultism, known as AMO (Astrology, Meta-psychology and Occultism).

Amado Crowley, Aleister Crowley's son, tells how early in 1940 'a group of strange men came to see Crowley', one being Louis de Wohl, who said that he and his colleagues 'would like you to help your country with the war effort'.[11] As a result of these talks Crowley was brought to London to be given details of the plans that were to be put to him. It was here that Ian Fleming was involved.

My father had a very high regard for Ian Fleming. He was
certainly an honourable man and never turned on my father,
once he had served government ends. I think Aleister Crowley
particularly liked Ian Fleming's attitude to life – *vivre pour vivre*
as the French say – and heartily approved of his joy in sex and
hedonism. Not that Fleming was in any way a debauched man.
He was quite strict with himself. I rather imagine it took a
handful of such fellows as Fleming and Dennis Wheatley to
draw Aleister Crowley to Admiral Godfrey's attention. It is also
my impression that Fleming was the intermediary in the early
stages between London and Lisbon. He made the arrangements
for the visit of the two Germans.[12]

From Crowley's meeting with Fleming and others in London
what was embarked on was known as Operation Mistletoe. The
phrase 'Mistletoe' was supposed to connect with the mythical
Balder, a handsome young god in Valhalla who was said to have
been killed when mistletoe was thrown after him in a game.
Crowley had become a member of the Order of the Golden Dawn
many years earlier and many leading Nazis were also members of
this occultist order. Crowley's son reports that 'we were set up to
meet two German officers, code-named "Kestrel" and "Sea
Eagle". The whole thing had been set up between the Romanian
Mission in London and its counterpart in Lisbon and was all very
hush-hush'.[13]

What happened after that as far as Aleister Crowley and
Fleming were involved remains to some extent a mystery, as
indeed it was intended to be. Here it was no longer a question of
astrology but of occult rites. These took place in Ashdown Forest
in Sussex. This much is confirmed by Amado Crowley, who
describes it as 'a high ritual', saying that the ceremony itself was
'long and complex . . . I have a very vivid memory of a dummy,
dressed in Nazi uniform, being sat on a throne-like chair. . . .
Most of the people there wore occult robes'. Amado Crowley says
that

Ian Fleming was present personally at the 'firework display' [as
Aleister called the ceremony in Ashdown Forest] and he was
very excited. For what it is worth I would say that *he was quite*

*confident that the whole bizarre process was going to work.*
Whether or not that suggests that he was an occultist himself, a
follower of Aleister Crowley, perhaps, I can only surmise. He
did one very charming thing which lends me some support to
the idea. When Aleister was dropped after the success of the
Hess affair, Fleming sent him a bottle of superb toilet water
from Trumps, or Trumpers, in Mayfair, along with a little note
which said:

> *King John*, IV, ii, 11: The passage read:
> To gild refined gold, to paint the lily,
> To throw a perfume on the violet,
> To smooth the ice, or add another hue
> Unto the rainbow, or with taper-light
> To seek the beauteous eye of heaven to garnish,
> Is wasteful and ridiculous excess.[14]

Certainly the Ashdown Forest rituals were linked to Hess and
the aim was to use it directly or indirectly to influence his actions. It
is still impossible to say how many temptations were being conjured up to impress Hess. Various ideas were thrown out to
induce him into believing that a visit to Britain would be worth
while. One was that the Duke of Windsor could be manipulated
into thinking he could make a peace deal with Hitler on condition
that Scotland gained independence and its own king, England
remaining under German control. At the same time Hess was
given to understand that he was regarded as a descendant of the
Hesse family, just like Lord Mountbatten.

However vital these imbroglios may have been in influencing
Hess's plans, the fact remains that on 10 May 1941 Hess flew to
Scotland. Almost immediately a blanket of silence was imposed
on the subject. It might be assumed that the British Government
would have been anxious to make use of Hess's arrival as a strong
propaganda coup, suggesting that Germany was ready to make
terms with Britain. Such was not the case. In the diaries of Joseph
Goebbels, Hitler's Minister of Propaganda, there were a number
of entries after Hess's flight to Britain expressing his bafflement
that no propaganda was being made about Hess. Then came this
enlightening comment on 22 June 1941: 'The Führer has high
hopes of the peace party in England. Otherwise, he claims, the

Hess affair would not have been so systematically killed by silence.'[15]

Nevertheless the reaction against all astrologers in Germany was swift and positive and this alone seems to show that Fleming's efforts had secured a success for Britain, even though it may have amounted to no more than valuable delaying tactics. Goebbels eventually set his propaganda machine in action against astrologers generally. One such article declared that Hess had been in poor health for many years and latterly had had recourse to hypnotists and astrologers. As a result, the Germans launched what became known as the *Aktion Hess*, which led to the arrest of hundreds of people, with astrologers at the top of the list.

Meanwhile for Fleming himself there was an unfortunate hiccup in his best-laid plans. It is even possible that he was encouraged to make these plans because of this. Peter Fleming had written a novel entitled *The Flying Visit*, published by Jonathan Cape in July 1940 and dedicated to his son Nicholas, with the inscription 'in the hope that this book, when he comes to read it, will be no longer even remotely topical'. The novel relates how Hitler, goaded by his desire to gloat over England, had himself flown over to that country one night, parachuting over the Chilterns and then finding himself on an estate not far from Nettlebed (ancestral home of the Fleming family) and gave himself up to a blonde agent, thus throwing the British Cabinet into confusion.

Was this an inspiration to Ian? Did it encourage his own daring plans? Ian actually urged his brother to go ahead with this idea for a book, doubtless seeing it as a possible means of signalling to the Germans that the British might talk if someone were lured to Britain – if not Hitler or Hess, then possibly Canaris. When Hess himself enacted Peter Fleming's fictitious ploy, no doubt it secretly delighted Ian, but the sheer coincidence of *The Flying Visit* narrative and Hess's arrival must at the same time have been somewhat embarrassing for him.

However, there is no evidence that the brothers colluded in Ian's secret operation. Peter Fleming stated long afterwards that Ian had not told him about 'this idea', which he described as 'a new legend about my brother'.[16] On the other hand, Sefton Delmer, who knew Ian Fleming well and had worked with him, commented: 'As an idea, inducing Hess to fly to England by means of astrological hocus-pocus – and the bait of the Duke of Hamilton – was something that might have appealed to Ian Fleming, or even to have been conceived by him. I am quite ready to believe that.'[17]

Later, anxious to stress that he had no knowledge of any such plans and, by implication, denying that his own novel had any connection with them, Peter Fleming affirmed that he did not believe 'the elaborate ruses were ever carried out, or even planned'.[18] None the less the undisputed fact remains that Fleming was anxious, once Hess had landed, to follow up his own hunches on the best way to handle him. He not only begged the authorities to allow Aleister Crowley to interview Hess, he even managed to persuade Crowley to offer his services for this purpose. Unfortunately the offer was not taken up. However, the first Intelligence officer to interview Hess was Brigadier Roy Firebrace, the first president of the Astrological Association of Great Britain, who had been tutored by a German astrologer.

In his biography of Professor Haushofer, Hess's adviser, Dr Rainier Hildebrandt states:

> Hess's astrological foible strengthened his own conviction that everything possible must be done and hazarded in order to end hostilities without delay because at the end of April and the beginning of May 1941. Hitler's astrological aspects were unusually malefic. Hess interpreted these aspects to mean that he personally must take the dangers that threaten the Führer upon his own shoulders in order to save Hitler and restore peace to Germany.[19]

Hess's chief astrological adviser had been Ernst Schulte-Strathaus, who later denied emphatically that Hess had chosen the date of 10 May 1941 to fly to Britain. Yet he was imprisoned by the Nazis because he was suspected of having given such advice. The organization of the plot on the part of Fleming in its careful attention to astrological detail was very thorough. In this respect the Swiss astrologer-agent who had faked the horoscope had done a good job. He knew what other astrological advice

Hess would be given – that Hitler and Germany were in danger around that vital date. He had only to incorporate their findings in his own report, with the additional advice that Hess should make the flight to Scotland.

It was a brilliant coup and Fleming deserves full credit for it, as also does the still mysterious Vanessa. Hess seems to have been toying with the idea of a flight to Britain long before May 1941. He himself declared that he had 'decided to fly shortly after a conversation with the Führer in June 1940. The delay was caused by difficulties in obtaining a machine and long-range equipment as well as unfavourable weather conditions. . . . I also postponed my flight for a certain time because our military setbacks in North Africa carried the danger that my sudden arrival in England might give rise to false interpretations as to my motives'.

The plot to lure Hess to Britain must have been going on for quite a long time. As a finale to this whole extraordinary story the text of Crowley's letter of 14 May 1941, inspired by Fleming, to the Director of Naval Intelligence, makes fascinating reading: 'If it is true that Herr Hess is much influenced by astrology and magick, my services might be of use to the Department [the NID], in case he should not be willing to do as you wish. Colonel J.F.C. Carter, Scotland House, SW1; Thos. N. Driberg, *Daily Express*; Karl J. Germer, 1007 Lexington Avenue, New York City could testify to my status and reputation in these matters.'

The name 'Thos. N. Driberg' may seem a surprising choice for a reference. Yet not only was he an informant for MI5 in those days, but when Crowley was in Germany spying on the notorious German agent, Gerald Hamilton, he often passed information on Hamilton back to London via Driberg.


This was not the only game involving occultism that Fleming played during his naval career. One of his most successful gambits of this kind was a cleverly worked out operation in which he manipulated individuals into carrying out tasks quite subconsciously, such as to pass on to the German Navy fake information about pendulum predictors. 'Pendulum prediction' had been used by certain occult practitioners before the war for finding hidden treasure and even missing people. It involved swinging a pendulum over a map of the area where the treasure or the missing person was supposed to be. By studying the swing of the pendulum, or so it was suggested, the location of the object of the search could be defined. The Nazis employed a number of pendulum swingers, one being Dr W. Gutberlet, a Munich physician, who had been a member of the Hitler circle in pre-war days (more information from Vanessa Hoffmann).

News filtered through to Britain of the establishment in Berlin of a Pendulum Institute which had close links with German Naval Intelligence. Some time after the round-up of the astrologers in Germany, following the flight of Hess to Britain, officers from German Naval Intelligence were given the task of interrogating some of the detainees. As a result, a number of detainees were released and employed by German Naval Intelligence. They used to meet at what became known as the Naval Branch of the Pendulum Institute – Intelligence X3, which was situated in an office in the Admiral von Schroederstrasse in Berlin. These people included astrologers, radiesthetic experts and mathematicians. The head of the Pendulum Intelligence team was Kapitan Hans Roeder of German Naval Intelligence.

Such activity may sound unworldly almost to the point of being farcical, but in the view of the German naval hierarchy the outcome of the war depended to a large extent on how devastating the U-boat campaign could be. Thus, any intelligence offering new targets for German submarines was welcomed, and the object of Intelligence X3 was to discover how pendulum detection could be used to pinpoint the positions and routes of enemy shipping with a view to their being sunk by U-boats.

Somehow Fleming, again operating on his own outside the NID and through some of his contacts in the twilight world of the occult, had managed to plant on the Germans the totally false story that the NID was employing pendulum practitioners in the Admiralty, where they would scan the charts with their pendulums and detect the positions of German U-boats. Very cleverly he had managed to leak this disinformation at a time when the British were sinking rather more submarines than usual. This success was therefore seen as proof of the efficacy of pendulum

practitioners and the Germans decided that the information must
be accurate. They believed that the pendulum practitioners fixed
the position of the U-boats and reported to Operations, who
immediately sent a signal to a warship to proceed to a certain
point and locate and sink submarines. Little did they know the
slow processes of the British Admiralty where, even if all this had
happened, by the time a signal had filtered through to the right
quarter, the submarines would almost certainly have been elsewhere already.

Yet there was some excuse for the Germans, because they had
been well aware of one of the most glaring failures of British
Naval Intelligence: that for the first three years of the war the NID
upheld the view that no U-boat could dive below six hundred feet,
as a result of which depth-charges were wrongly set and consequently often wasted. It was not until the second half of 1942 that
the NID was eventually able to convince the Admiralty that
U-boats could go much deeper. Thus, when there were more
U-boat sinkings, German Naval Intelligence believed that these
might be the result of pendulum swinging and not because of
better settings of depth-charges.

Kapitan Roeder was himself convinced of this and he decided to
investigate the use of pendulum techniques and to employ them
for attacks on enemy shipping. Herr Ludwig Straniak of Salzburg
claimed to be able to locate the position of a ship by holding a
pendulum over a photograph of it and then scanning charts with a
pendulum. Straniak was invited to join the Pendulum Institute
team in Berlin and German Naval Intelligence agreed to set up
the Pendulum Institute on the island of Sylt, which location, it was
hoped, would be removed from the disturbances of bombings and
the noise of a capital city. So absorbed were they in their experiments that it never dawned on them that the story of what the
NID was doing might be false.[20]

When Hess was taken into custody by the British and Fleming had
failed to have him interviewed by Crowley, that was the end of the
Hess story as far as Fleming was concerned. That the full story
about Hess has not been told and may never be told seems

increasingly likely. True though it is that secret files on the Hess affair were released for inspection in June 1992, the large amount of material then produced told us little that we did not know already. In effect, all that the released material did was to confirm what we had been told during and after the war. It still left a huge number of questions unanswered. As far as this chapter is concerned, the sole item of interest was the revelation that 'among the books he [Hess] received from home in the spring of 1943 were a defence of astrology and several historical novels. . . . Letters seem to have been held for several months both by the British and German censorships, some arriving six months late'.[21]

But for the fact that Fleming and I shared certain knowledge about William Otto Lucas and those of the latter's contacts mentioned in this chapter, it is almost certain that I should not have known this story of the attempt to lure Hess to Britain. A meeting of Secret Service personnel and others was presided over by the late Sir Maurice Oldfield, then head of MI6, in the mid-seventies, to consider whether certain facts concerning the Hess affair should be released to the public. The suggestion has been made that such a disclosure would settle the quesion as to whether it was Hess himself or a substitute for the deputy Führer who parachuted into Scotland. The decision then taken seems to have been that the full story on Hess would not be revealed until the year 2017. Despite the so-called 'revelations' of 1992, so disappointing and dull, it appears that this is still the official view.

Meanwhile the whole story is, if anything, more puzzling than it was prior to Hess's mysterious death in Spandau Prison. The main questions to be asked now are (1) Was it Hess or his 'double' who came to Britain? (2) Did Hess (or his double) commit suicide by hanging himself in Spandau Prison, or was he murdered? (3) If he was murdered, who gave the order and who carried it out?

# 6

## No. 30 Assault Unit

'My Red Indians,' Fleming called them. They brought colour
(and fury) into Fleming's life and he, the most generous, least
malicious, most gay, most melancholy man I ever knew, in
turn brought colour (and occasional fury) into the lives of
others.[1]

To be cramped inside the overcrowded offices of Naval
Intelligence probably irked Fleming a great deal: he was
essentially a man of action who liked to see such action carried out
personally. Where he was fortunate was that under Admiral
Godfrey he had a master who was in many ways just as restless
and unconventional as he was himself.

It was as a result of his impressing on Godfrey the need for the
kind of assault unit which the Germans had used in Crete that the
DNI gave full support to the creation of what became known as
No. 30 Assault Unit, or 30 AU. Fleming was given the task of
organizing it. Initially it was employed in the Middle East, working with the Eighth Army under the dual command of Quentin
Riley, a pre-war Polar explorer, and Dunstan Curtis, who had
commanded the leading ship in the commando raid on St Nazaire.
The unit's first major operation was to have been carried out
during the disastrous raid on Dieppe, but they never got ashore.
This was, Fleming declared afterwards, 'the unhappiest memory
of the war, for there was I, absolutely impotent as a spectator of
the whole affair from a warship'.

The raid was launched on 19 August 1942, when a Combined
Operations expedition of British and Canadian forces in 252 ships
and small landing-craft set ashore on the French coast more than

six thousand men for what Churchill guardedly called 'a re-
connaisance in force', but which Colonel C.F. Stacey, in the
Canadian official history of the war, described as 'tactically an
almost complete failure, for we suffered extremely heavy losses
and attained few of our objectives'.[2]

Fleming had purely an observer's role during the Dieppe raid,
which must have been exceedingly frustrating for him. In his
papers in Reading University he makes the comment that 'my
nearly first piece of descriptive prose was about the Dieppe Raid,
which I did for the Weekly Intelligence report for the Fleet'. His
enthusiasm for the cause of 30 AU was, however, fully revived in
Operation Torch, the North African landings, in which it single-
handedly captured the Italian Naval Headquarters in Algiers. The
unit was eventually brought back to Britain to prepare for the
full-scale invasion of Europe and Fleming then had complete
control in the background, often going to watch his 'Red Indians'
in training.

By this time the NID had a new director, Rear-Admiral E.G.N.
Rushbrooke, a quite different officer from Godfrey, very serious-
minded, who was given the unfortunate nickname of 'Rush-
Admiral Rearbrook'. It was about this time that Fleming had
attached to him the young American naval officer, Lt Alan
Schneider, who comments:

> As time went on we got to be quite close while engaged in
> planning for the invasion. We were both ideas men and would
> come up with all sorts of hair-brained schemes, making sure that
> someone else would have to carry them out. . . . We used to
> talk to each other in German – mine was just like English to me
> then and his was equal or better. We used to get some odd
> looks when we were out in public speaking German. . . . It just
> wasn't a normal thing in wartime London. As a matter of fact
> Ian said that a head waiter had once called Scotland Yard to
> arrest him, causing a flap at the Admiralty.[3]

This was a reference to the occasion when Fleming, who liked
occasionally to cock a snook at the Establishment, took a German
prisoner of war to a West End restaurant for dinner, at the same
time seeking information from him.

Alan Schneider spent a great deal of time with Fleming and 30 AU.

> It was inevitable that something of Ian's control should pass to others, but he made an indelible impression on them. . . . Ian's responsibility was to prepare the Security Plan for the British Navy and mine was the same for the United States Navy. Ian and I had at this time a pass we both prized highly. It was in English, French, German and Russian, signed by General Eisenhower. It is said we were not to be questioned by anyone at any time, and all were ordered to give us immediate assistance, including all methods of transportation. . . . I covered the south coast of England from Falmouth to Plymouth and Portsmouth. Ian took the rest of the coast.[4]

In all this planning for Operation Overlord, the code-name for the invasion of France by the Allies, Fleming built up his own dossier of intelligence which he somehow managed to get out of Germany. From such highly personal intelligence as he acquired he became convinced that the Germans were making fabricated parts for one-man submarines in both France and Germany, transporting the parts by train to assembly points and getting them ready for the invasion. Then he decided that if he could find a train that was actually carrying these prefabricated parts of the submarines, he could use 30 AU to investigate and prove that his surmise was right. 'He got the mission approved,' says Alan Schneider, 'but to his consternation he was not allowed to go.' Fleming detailed Schneider to take his place in 30 AU and a train was blown up when it was in a tunnel. Schneider, who keeps the name-plate of the train on his office wall, was injured and could not be taken back straight away. He had to hide in a farmhouse in Normandy for a while and returned to England only six months before the invasion.

Schneider very soon realized that it would not be long before he landed in France again, because on one of their occasional pre-arranged meetings at the Seven Stars Hotel in Totnes, Fleming informed him that he was to go in with 30 AU on D-Day on the Arromanches beachhead. The Assault Unit's task was to reach the German radar station there before the enemy had time to destroy it. The aim was to capture the log-books, code-books and anything else of value. A British motor torpedo-boat was to transport Schneider there and bring him back safely.

Intelligence acquired by 30 AU was used in the entire briefings for D-Day. For example, a detailed description was provided of the enemy positions which the guns of HMS *Ramillies* was supposed to silence. It read thus: 'Coordinate 155 G, 25007. Originally open emplacements, heavily earthbanked. Four casements uncovered. Range falls approximately 2,000 yards short of Manvieux and east limits of beach, but covers swept area for gunfire support. Casemate construction started in March, laid out radically facing bearing 347 degrees.'

30 AU went in to the beach in landing-craft, Schneider following in the torpedo-boat, awaiting a signal that the radar station had been captured. An invaluable haul of materials was secured and four hours later it was delivered to the Admiralty in London. From then onwards the invasion of France and the follow-up was a total success, achieved with the minimum loss of life. Meanwhile Fleming was itching to get into action himself. His chance came following a conference between Rear-Admiral Rushbrooke, the ONI Commodore Tully Shelly of the US Embassy in London, Fleming and Schneider. The outcome of this conference was the launching of a plan to speed up the Allies' advance in France by linking up with General George S. Patton in Normandy and for 30 AU to operate in this area.

Fleming, along with Schneider, flew to France. They had talks with General Patton, a formidable and highly effective soldier but not – as is well known – an easy man to deal with. He disliked the title 30 Assault Unit and after some argument said he would accept the unit only if the name was changed to Task Force 30. From then onwards real progress was made and perhaps the newly named Task Force's most astonishing find was a huge installation under construction, which puzzled everyone at first. Eventually it was learned that this was the beginning of a launching-pad intended for firing the intercontinental ballistic missiles Hitler was having made, which were to be aimed at the east coast of the United States. Had the pad remained for a few more months in German hands, such an attack would have been possible. It was Germany's ambitious development of something bigger than the V1s and V2s, which they directed across the Channel at Britain.

Ian and his American colleague gradually made their way to Paris for the liberation of that city. On the way, says Schneider, 'girls began climbing on the vehicles. One wrapped herself around Ian as the jeep moved on. One climbed down the turret in my armoured car. They were everywhere, and when we got to the end of town, the column slowed and they all got off, blowing kisses and shouting to us to come back'.[5]

Ian's Assault Unit or Task Force came to be called 'Fleming's private Army' by some. There is no question that its reconnaissance work in the months and days before D-Day enabled thousands of lives to be saved, probably tens of thousands. Thanks to Fleming the Force maintained among its members a happy-go-lucky, piratical spirit with a dislike of bureaucratic discipline. One RNVR officer, for example, captured three hundred Germans and their radar station with the aid of only half a dozen ratings and Marines.

Yet another highly effective operation, which was planned by Commander Sir George Binney, RNVR, the late Vice-Admiral Sir Norman Denning and Ian Fleming at Binney's London flat, was Operation Moonshine. This was discussed in the autumn of 1943 and resulted in five motor gunboats being disarmed and converted into mini-merchantmen. Flying the red ensign, their job was to bring back 358 tons of ball-bearings and other Swedish products in nine round trips between Hull and Gothenburg. Only one craft was lost.

Fleming also indulged in certain disinformation ploys against the Japanese in the Far East. The aim in 1944 was to enable British and Americans to concentrate on the invasion of Europe and to delay action in the Far East until that was accomplished. Thus the plan was to feed the Japanese with propaganda which suggested that the build-up of Allied Forces in India and the Pacific Ocean area was far greater than it was. Fleming created a purely fictitious group of double agents for this purpose: they were known as Hiccoughs, a very typical Fleming code-name!

One of the great puzzles in this period was how Fleming

managed to handle so many highly complicated operations at one
and the same time and covering all parts of the world. He continued, for example, his soundings on Admiral Canaris and even
gave serious thought to having him kidnapped. He would have
much preferred to lure Canaris rather than Hess to Britain, but here
he was up against objections on all sides, the Foreign Office and
some influential people in the Secret Service and, of course, all
those politicians on both sides of the Atlantic who were frightened
of upsetting Stalin. Hovering in the background, tactically placed
to serve two masters – the SIS and the Soviet Union – was Kim
Philby as head of the Iberian Section of MI6. It was Philby who
sabotaged so many attempted overtures to Canaris and his aides.

Canaris worked against both communism and Hitler while pre-
cariously maintaining control of the *Abwehr*. Reinhardt Gehlen,
who became intelligence chief of the German Army in 1942 and at
the end of the war brought his files with him when surrendering to
the Americans, had this to say about the head of the *Abwehr*:

> Canaris was a convinced opponent of the Nazis. Like General
> Beck he suffered deeply from the internal conflict between the
> military oath he had sworn in God's name and his opposition to
> the regime. . . . I recall a long private talk I had with Canaris in
> 1942 in which he discoursed at length on the concept of treason,
> and concluded that I could be justified, given the exceptional
> circumstances of the war Germany was now fighting. . . .
> Canaris added that the traitor must recognise that only one
> thing would guarantee justice to the conspirators – the plot must
> succeed. . . . Canaris acted accordingly, gathering into the
> *Abwehr* many people endangered by their political belief,
> shielding them from the grasp of the Gestapo.[6]

One of the earliest links between Canaris and British Naval
Intelligence was Don Juan March, a Spanish millionaire and
former head of a smuggling ring that had been won over to the
side of the NID in the First World War. When Juan March
escaped from Spain to Gibraltar during the Spanish Civil War, it
was the NID who tipped him off and arranged for his escape from
the Alcara de Henares prison where he had been held on charges
of alleged tobacco smuggling. This paved the way to considerable

co-operation between March and the British in the Second World War. One of the shrewdest minds in the Gibraltar section of the NID during the war, and a great friend of Fleming's, was Don Gomez-Beare, who became British naval attaché in Madrid. He was always in close contact with March and, as a result, was able to pass on information about Canaris. 'At times,' Gomez-Beare told me years later, 'it seemed as though Canaris was practically inviting the NID to open secret negotiations with him. But with Canaris one couldn't be quite sure what his motives were. In retrospect we might have done much more and so shortened the war. The pity was that Godfrey was taken away from the NID at a vital stage of the war. Fleming always regretted this'.

Canaris seemed to regret it, too. A message which Fleming received from Vanessa Hoffmann concerning Canaris late in 1943 stated that he found the NID 'not as circumspect as in Admiral Hall's day . . . how can you deal with an organization which changes its directors so frequently?' Prior to this Room 39 had been given various reports on the Germans setting up observation posts on both sides of the Strait of Gibraltar and on Alboran Island from which direct wireless communication was maintained with Berlin, Paris and Madrid. The Germans were then preparing sites on Spanish territory west of the Bay of Gibraltar to install infra-red apparatus and radar. Yet it was not until Fleming acquired more detailed information from his own sources that action was taken. From then on he played a leading role in what was known as thwarting the Gibraltar Plot. His personal order was that 'the Germans' detailed and deadly watch must be frustrated'.[7]

Out went orders through Fleming that Gomez-Beare and Commander (later Captain) Alan Hillgarth, also naval attaché in Madrid, were to impress upon the Spaniards the need for this German operation to be stopped. German archives have since revealed that these overtures bore results and that there was an agreement between Franco and Canaris to cancel it. One of Fleming's other vital contacts regarding Canaris was Cedric Salter, then correspondent of the *Daily Express* in Istanbul. Early in 1943 Salter learned that the US naval attaché in Istanbul, George Earle, had received a message from Canaris. The admiral wanted to know what kind of peace terms the United States would be prepared to consider. Allen Dulles, who was in Berne at the time, received similar soundings from Gisevius, an agent of Canaris in Switzerland. When finally Canaris learned of the Allies' totally ridiculous 'unconditional surrender' demands at the Casablanca Conference, he warned that 'we shall all have to pay for this one day, and the price America and Britain will pay will be just as great as for Germany. Unconditional surrender means nothing other than victory for the Soviet Union'. This message or warning – call it what one will – from Canaris was passed to Salter, who later confirmed its wording to me.

From time to time Canaris made trips to Algeciras in Spain, just across the border from Gibraltar. On some occasions these were semi-official, on others they were totally secret. On one of these visits Canaris dropped hints that he might have talks with 'a certain naval person', adding that: 'If your people care to look up your records, you will find that you obtained some very important intelligence in Stockholm from a Hamburg source that led to the sinking of the *Bismarck* and you very nearly ignored the true purport of this.' The person to whom Canaris then spoke was none other than Don Gomez-Beare, who at that time was out of uniform. 'I always thought the "certain naval person" he mentioned was Ian Fleming,' he told me several years later. 'The trouble with Canaris was that he talked in riddles very often.'

It was about this time that Fleming appears to have lost touch with Vanessa Hoffmann. Certainly as far as her Swiss intermediaries were concerned there was total silence from her for the rest of the war and, as she has never been heard of since, it may well be that she was liquidated. Tragically, her actual identity remains a mystery even to this day. There is even some doubt as to whether her name was Hoffmann, which was how she was known to Fleming and his friends when she was in Switzerland and Austria before the war. But when she disappeared, some rather disparaging remarks were made about her, even by her intermediaries in Switzerland. Possibly they thought she was helping Germany more than the Allies and that this was the reason for her silence. Wythe Williams received a message from his contact 'Clara' that 'Vanessa might have been part Irish and part British', whatever that may mean. One suggestion was that

she was an Irish nationalist, but that seems most unlikely.
Fleming, who tried to trace her, believed that probably the
Gestapo had caught her and that they had put out false stories to
be leaked to the British in order to discredit her.

Up to the last Fleming toyed on his own, as far as one can
judge, with the idea of kidnapping Canaris on one of his visits to
Algeciras. Much later in the war Canaris planned yet another
incognito visit to Spain. Yet when he set out on his journey he was
astonished to learn that the Spanish authorities would not allow
him to cross the frontier. An NID agent and a friend of Fleming's
had been waiting to have talks with him on that occasion. It was
never clear whether this visit was sabotaged by some mischievous
false information given to the Spaniards by Kim Philby of the
Iberian Section of the SIS, or warnings given by the Germans.

Early in April 1945 Canaris was arrested and garrotted by the
Gestapo on Hitler's orders.

For Fleming, the war ended when he made a journey into
Germany to capture German naval archives which were left in the
charge of an elderly admiral at the castle of Tambach in the
Württemberg Forest. This successful mission ended in all the
archives being brought back to London. However, his somewhat
desperate efforts to obtain news of Vanessa brought him no news
at all. He managed to find one old friend of hers, whose only
surmise was that Vanessa was either dead or had left Germany.

In recent years a story has been circulated in London and
elsewhere to the effect that early in 1945 Fleming went on a
clandestine mission to Germany to trace where Nazi loot had been
hidden and at the same time to kidnap Martin Bormann, then
Hitler's deputy. Indeed, some sources have even elaborated on
this story to claim that Fleming brought Bormann back to London
and enabled him to live there in secrecy under a new name! This
latter version of the story is certainly untrue, as Bormann's remains were subsequently dug up many years later near the
Weidenhammer Bridge in Berlin not far from Hitler's bunker.
Bormann is assumed to have been hit by enemy fire as he was
trying to escape.

Nor does there seem to be the slightest evidence for the story of an attempt to rescue Bormann. Lord Dacre (then Hugh Trevor-Roper), who was stationed in Germany and working closely with British Intelligence in September 1945, says that 'if there had been a hunt for Bormann in April–June of that year, as alleged, I think (indeed, feel sure) that I would have learned about it, but I never heard a syllable about any such operation'.[8] Antony Terry, for many years Kemsley Newspapers correspondent in Germany, dismisses such reports as nonsense, not least on the grounds that before Bormann's remains were dug up he had been sent on 'a wild goose chase to South America to find Bormann'.[9]

Despite Admiral Godfrey's claim that 'Ian was a war winner', Fleming received no decoration from the British for his services in the Second World War. It is true that he did not get along nearly so well with Rear-Admiral Rushbrooke as he had with Godfrey. This to some extent seems to be confirmed by Alan Schneider who states that 'Commodore Shelly [his chief Intelligence officer] told me that Rushbrooke had said that Ian wasn't able to follow up on things very well. I took his telling me this as some kind of warning'.[10]

Despite this 'warning', Schneider came to have a high regard for Fleming. At the end of the war he was posted to Germany, his target for operations being the German Naval Headquarters (*Der Oberkommando der Kriegsmarine*). Here he found a bunch of Iron Crosses, one of which he sent to Fleming.

> He wrote me a letter and thanked me for it and said that the only medals or decorations he had received for the entire war had been foreign ones. One was the German Iron Cross I sent him and the other was the Commander's Cross of the Order of the Dannebrog from Denmark. He had received this one because a subordinate in Room 39 had been asked by a friend in the Danish Government for the names of some people deserving gratitude and he had put Ian's name on it. This was so hard to understand. He certainly deserved medals and decorations in profusion.[11]

Fleming's former DNI, Godfrey, had equally been denied recognition for his services. This may have been a result of

Churchill's vendetta against him. Fleming continued to treat his lack of recognition as a joke, whatever he may have felt privately. When his friend Philip Brownrigg was awarded the CMG, Fleming sent him a copy of one of his books inscribed: 'To Philip, CMG, from Ian (failed OBE)'.

At the very end of the war Fleming had to do some hard thinking about his future career. Should he return to the City, carry on in the Navy, or move into some other section of Intelligence? The City did not appeal to him, nor did he see himself in a peace-time Navy. There were certain approaches from friends in the Secret Service which he seriously considered. He had been closely associated with the head of MI6, Major-General Sir Stewart Menzies, throughout the war and each had had a desire to win over Admiral Canaris as an ally despite objections from within the Foreign Office, which seemed desperately anxious not to offend or upset the Russians. But Fleming realized that work for the Secret Service would not guarantee him an adequate income. In one of his books he made a Soviet Intelligence officer pay tribute to British secret agents by stressing that they did splendid work at great risks for very little payment.

Without doubt Fleming knew that he had made enemies as well as friends in his wartime career. Many were jealous of the man they most unfairly called 'the Chocolate Sailor': he was the kind of glamorous figure who delighted women but was envied by men. Had his friend Major-General Sir Colin Gubbins become a key figure in the SIS when his organization, the SOE, was disbanded, Fleming might have gone into Intelligence. He had all the qualities for a splendid future leader: he possessed imagination and was full of ideas, he handled staff splendidly, he had courage and love of action and, above all, he was a first-class administrator. One former MI6 senior member told me: 'Had he joined us he could very easily have become ultimately a very senior member. He would have made an outstanding 'C' [head of MI6], far better than some of those who succeeded Menzies.'

# 7

## *Jamaican Paradise*

It is the nearest ear, nose and throat clinic on the right. Hence
Goldeneye, Nose and Throat![1]

Fleming had long had a dream of creating for himself a
hideaway home in a far-off place. During the Second World
War he had occasionally made brief stops in the West Indies. The
Caribbean area appealed to him, and so did the pastimes offered
by this part of the world, especially underwater swimming.

It may seem surprising that he found time to practise such
pursuits in wartime, but that this must be true was borne out by
William Plomer who claimed that 'it was Admiral Godfrey who
introduced him [Fleming] to the delights of underwater
swimming, when it was much less familiar than it is now. It
seemed an activity exactly made for him. It was athletic, it was not
without its hazards, and it offered the discovery of a hidden world
of fascinating mysteries. Discovery, I think, is the key-word: Ian
was a great finder out'.[2]

Such opportunities were presented, though briefly, when a
high-level Anglo-American naval intelligence conference was held
for five days at Kingston, Jamaica, in 1942. Sinkings in the
Caribbean had then reached their peak, some two hundred ships
having been torpedoed by the Germans in a single month. It was
then that Fleming decided he wanted to make a home in Jamaica
after the war.

From then on underwater exploration became a new and
exhilarating hobby. Fleming would make his underwater
excursions, equipped with mask and spears, sometimes alone, but
often in company, occasionally with women. He used a spear-gun

111

for fishing. But he also interested himself in the fauna and flora of the Caribbean environment. Occasionally, but only to those who were keenly interested in such topics, he would expound with considerable knowledge on rare types of sea shells and tropical birds. He not only knew Jamaica thoroughly, but other parts of the Caribbean such as the Bahamas. Once, along with his friends, Ivar Bryce, Arthur Verney, President of the Society for the Preservation of the Flamingo in the Bahamas and Dr Robert Cushman Murphy, curator of marine birds for the American museums of natural history, he went on an expedition to the island of Inagua in the Bahamas. On this island was a large lagoon, some hundred square miles in area: Fleming followed the usual drill for exploring this lagoon, which was to wade across it, pushing a shallow-draught boat.

Ivar Bryce was asked to find the dream hide-out home for Ian Fleming. Eventually he discovered a fourteen-acre strip of land on the north coast of Jamaica, between the coast road and the sea, close to the village and harbour of Oracabessa. 'The coast here was high above the water, along a stretch of cliff about forty feet in height. . . . The view was enchanting – a bay of clear aquamarine protected by a broad and tangled reef,' says Bryce.[3] It was an ideal site for indulging in underwater exploration.

Fleming bought the site for £2,000 and on it he built a modest house, somewhat spartanly planned and certainly not to everyone's taste, but ideal for himself. 'Here on a headland Ian Fleming has built a house called Goldeneye that might serve as a model for new houses in the tropics,' wrote Patrick Leigh Fermor in 1950. 'Trees surround it on all sides except the sea, which it almost overhangs.'[4]

Noël Coward, who also had a house on the north coast of Jamaica, took a somewhat different view of Goldeneye. He said of it: '. . . all you Flemings revel in discomfort'.[5] This comment may have been induced by the fact that the house had a lack of baths and window-panes and that it was sparsely furnished. The dining alcove had hard, upright benches and planters' chairs. At one time the house had no curtains. Bryce was the first visitor to Goldeneye and Noël Coward the second.

It has been said that Oracabessa is Spanish for Goldenhead and that this is why Fleming chose the name Goldeneye for his holiday retreat. However, Bryce, who should certainly know the real facts, told me that Fleming named Goldeneye after the code-name of a wartime operation conceived and led by him across the English Channel to search for and destroy any enemy look-out post on the occupied shore of France. This is correct in that Goldeneye was the code-name for a NID operation in the war, though this concerned a Spanish operation master-minded by Fleming and not one across the Channel. Donald McLachlan, in his book *Room 39*, states that 'Goldeneye was the code word given in these measures, and later adopted as the name of the house that Commander Ian Fleming built for himself in Jamaica'.

While planning his Jamaican retreat Fleming was also giving serious thought to his future. In one sense the choice of a site for the retreat was linked with this. He had no doubt that from now on Britain would have closer ties to the United States than ever before and that he needed to visit the Western world regularly to keep in touch with his numerous new-found friends there – in the United States and the Caribbean. His wartime career had been an undoubted success, in some ways beyond his wildest dreams, and for this reason he hesitated as to what his peace-time career should be.

From what he told some of his friends, Fleming had had the idea of writing a novel even in the war years. Equally it is certain that the purchase of a home in the West Indies was partly made with this objective: Goldeneye was a retreat in which to work as much as to relax and play. It was not only Jamaica that he adored, but Haiti with its voodoo and strange cults and the many smaller islands which he liked to explore.

In the early days at Goldeneye Fleming spent much of his time navigating the waters around his home and, equipped with mask, fins and spears, exploring the subterranean crannies of the reef in which barracudas abounded. Meanwhile he arranged for paths to be cut out, one to each limit of the boundaries of his estate. At the end of each he built an octagonal summer-house. Initially, his routine in Jamaica was to rise at 7.30 a.m., swim out to the reef and inspect the weather conditions for the day and then return to the house for a large glass of orange juice. Later on, when he started writing, he would sit at his typewriter from 10 a.m. until lunch-time, working at a desk in his bedroom. Much later on, he replaced his old typewriter with a gold-plated model. Sometimes he showed off the new model with almost schoolboyish enthusiasm, or displayed it as a kind of joke against himself.

Fleming made no pretence of being a gardener. He hated plants in pots and disliked flowers in the house. Even in his office in London there was a strict ban on flowers. Presiding in an efficient and understanding manner over the whole household, however, was Violet, the Jamaican housekeeper, who cooked, cleaned, washed and sorted out all manner of problems for Fleming. She was devoted to her employer, though she must have found some of his guests eccentric if not troublesome. There was one occasion when Violet's 'Lordie, lordie!' must have come loud and clear on discovering that the novelist, Rosamond Lehmann, had thrown a live octopus into Fleming's bedroom when she became annoyed about something.

An early visitor to Goldeneye was Anne Rothermere, the wife of the late Lord Rothermere, proprietor of the *Daily Mail* and other newspapers. Lady Rothermere had originally been married to Lord O'Neill, one of Fleming's bridge and golfing companions. He had been killed in action in Italy in 1944. Esmond, Lord Rothermere, had been married to Margaret Hunan Redhead, from whom he was divorced in 1938. As early as 1941 Anne O'Neill, as she then was, tried to persuade Esmond that either they must get married or part, and as a result they went through the rigmarole of providing evidence for divorce in Bournemouth. However, as Anne later admitted, 'Ian told me I was behaving badly and that I must return to Shane [her husband].'[6]

Though Anne and Ian had met regularly for lunches and dinners on their own during the war and seemed to be on the best of terms, it was to Esmond Rothermere that she became married in 1945. However, she still kept in close touch with Fleming, often staying with him at a house named White Cliffs at St Margaret's Bay, near Dover, which was lent to them by Noël Coward. Coward and Fleming first met in 1948 and they became great friends, spending much time together both in England and Jamaica. White Cliffs was situated on the shoreline in a sheltered position at the foot of the cliffs and had unobstructed views of the Channel and the French coast. Today it is known as Mermaid Cottage. Eventually Coward decided that though this retreat had given him great pleasure, he had 'never really worked well there'.[7] He thereupon sold the house to Fleming.

In 1948 Anne Rothermere gave birth to a daughter who lived for only a few hours. Rothermere was told that Fleming was the father, but whether this was the case is uncertain. None the less Rothermere decreed that his wife was not to meet Fleming for the next six months. During the late summer of 1948, while I was a correspondent based on the then International Zone of Tangier, Fleming requested me to return to London for a brief visit. I casually mentioned to him that in Tangier the easiest divorces of anywhere in the world were then obtainable. I think that Fleming must have brought up this subject in the first place, as I should have been unlikely to mention it otherwise. Probably he subtly started off by asking me about the laws of the International Zone. The reason I recall this incident is that Fleming immediately seized upon the subject and instructed me to go to the Foreign Office to make sure that a Tangier divorce would be recognized by British authorities. This I did and was able to confirm that it was the case. It now seems that at that time Rothermere would not bring himself to undertake divorce proceedings and that Ian and Anne were possibly interested in obtaining a divorce despite his opposition.

Two years previously Anne Rothermere had done her utmost to put people off the scent of her secret affair with Fleming. Sometimes this was done in the most mischievous fashion, even to the extent of involving mutual friends. For example, she is supposed to have supplied the information upon which Cholly Knickerbocker, the newspaper columnist, wrote the following story in the *Journal-American* in 1946: 'Fleming is a sort of Beau Brummel of the islands [he was referring to the West Indies]. At one time he was rumoured to be Millicent Huddleston Rogers' hottest romance. But the Standard Oil millionairess showed it couldn't be that serious because she left Jamaica shortly afterwards to join Clark Gable in Hollywood. . . . But to get back to the Duchess of Westminster and Captain [*sic*] Fleming. How serious this flirtation might be is hard to tell.'

The Duchess of Westminster was a friend of both Ian and Anne. Meanwhile Anne Rothermere was beginning to cause her husband some concern on account of her high spending. 'Esmond has no dollars and is appalled at my extravagance,' she wrote to Fleming while on a visit to the United States in 1948.[8] At the same time she was doing all she could to get persons of her own choice into key positions on her husband's newspapers. It was Anne Rothermere who schemed to have Frank Owen appointed editor of the *Daily Mail*. This much was noted by *Time* magazine, which commented that '*Mail* men gossiped that Owen's promotion was plotted by Anne Rothermere, who keeps a bright and calculating eye on her easy-going husband's affairs'.[9]

From the beach at Goldeneye Ian and Anne sometimes went snorkeling together and exploring the nearby cave which was full of sand-martins. Sometimes Loelia, Duchess of Westminster, acted as chaperone to Anne on such visits. Some years later Fleming wrote that 'my daily occupation in Jamaica is spear-fishing and underwater exploring, but, after five years of it, I didn't want to kill any more fish except barracudas and the occasional monster fish, and I knew the underwater terrain like the back of my hand. But my mental hands were idle'.[10]

Coward, who lived at a house named Firefly in Jamaica, was a frequent visitor, and Fleming also maintained a friendship with Lord Beaverbrook, who had a house in Montego Bay. Other occasional visitors to Goldeneye were Evelyn Waugh and René McColl, the *Daily Express* writer. McColl told an amusing story about Fleming and Waugh:

> Fleming told Waugh that he knew he was on the ball when he became excited by what he was writing about. 'Oh,' said Waugh, 'and what were you writing about this morning?' 'I was describing Bond's latest girl,' said Fleming.
> 'Humph,' grunted Waugh, 'and did she excite you?'
> 'Well, no,' rejoined Fleming, 'she didn't.'
> 'Then back to your typewriter and start all over again' thundered Waugh.[11]

Fleming took a lively interest in almost everything about Jamaica. In many ways it was what one might call a romantic interest, as though he wished to weave a spell around his own environment. This much was vividly expressed in an article about the island which he had published in *Horizon* in 1947. In it he referred to the natives of Jamaica as 'a kindly and humorous people in the most beautiful large tropical island in the world'. Some of Fleming's finest prose went into that article, in which he captured the particular magic that Jamaica somehow always seems to produce at every twist and turn along its roads or out in its fields and forests. One single foreign word in the article seemed to evoke the peculiar, almost decadent charm of the island – *dégringolade*, a French adjective which has several meanings, but which by its very sound tells one far more than any English equivalent.

During his early years in Jamaica Fleming found an ally and useful guide to life in what was then still a British colony in Lady Huggins, wife of the Governor of Jamaica. Lady Molly, as she was generally known, was not at all the typical Empire pioneer. There was nothing austere about her; indeed she was as glamorous as any of her three charming daughters and her serenely sunny smile was haloed by a mass of golden-blonde curls. She was idolized by the Jamaicans who, when she was about to leave the island at the end of her husband's term of office, wanted to buy her a piece of land so that she could build a house there and come back to Jamaica to live.

One of the many hobbies that Fleming developed as a result of his journeys in the Caribbean was treasure-hunting. He admitted to me once that it was something he had been enthralled by as a child and that he had never quite grown out of the 'addiction', as he called it. One story of treasure-hunting which had fascinated him from an early age was that of the Oak Island Treasure Pit and the loot which Captain William Kidd was supposed to have secreted before he was executed at Wapping in 1701. In 1795 three young men took a canoe through the waters of Mahone Bay off the coast of Nova Scotia. This bay contained more than three hundred small islands. The men landed on one of them, called Oak Island because it had a single oak tree growing on it. As a result of their suspicions that somebody had buried treasure deep down beneath the oak tree the Oak Island Treasure Company was formed. Despite extensive researches, nothing was found. Then in

1909 four young men raised £2,000 and went to Oak Island with a drill: one of these men was Franklin Delano Roosevelt, later to become President of the United States.

Fleming had delved into the story of Captain Kidd's buried treasure over the years. He learned that there were other possible sites for this treasure apart from Oak Island, most notably in the Caribbean or the China Sea. I do recall that some time in 1950 he learned that Captain Kidd's treasure maps, drawn by his own hand, had been found in Mrs Kidd's workbox and that they were up for sale. Fleming asked to make inquiries on the subject and to make detailed notes for him. I learned that a Mrs Elizabeth Dick, of Eastbourne, had been left the maps together with a collection of piratical mementoes ranging from pieces of eight and doubloons to cutlasses and muskets by a solicitor to whom she was housekeeper. The largest map had been checked by experts who declared that the handwriting tallied with known specimens of Kidd's handwriting. There was also a reference to a stone on Oak Island with Captain Kidd's name on it.

Fleming was quite excited about this information and he told me he believed that Kidd had left various amounts of treasure in at least two or three different places. The maps were put up for auction, but whether he made a bid for them successfully or otherwise I do not know. While this fascination for buried treasure stories may have begun as a passion for romantic adventure, latterly I felt that some of his research into the subject was linked to his novel writing. One example of this was his novel *Live and Let Die* (1954), in which he told of Bloody Morgan's cave and the hunt for his treasure.[12] Of this book Fleming wrote in his own blurb: 'I make no pretensions to sensitive writing about unhappy childhoods, the flutterings of virgin hearts in suburban tearooms, or the underprivileged of Tulse Hill. I write adventure stories designed to take one's mind as far as possible away from these things. Some reviewers find my plots fantastic. I disagree with them. The fantastic occurs every day. . . . I never write about places I have not seen.'

Another character who fascinated Fleming was the poet John Gawsworth, who styled himself the 'King of Redonda'. In 1880 a trader had landed on Redonda, a gaunt, tall rock jutting out into the Caribbean Sea, its single saleable commodity being guano, used for phosphate production. He claimed the island for himself and presented it as a birthday gift to his son, who later became M.P. Shiel, the Irish romantic novelist. Shiel, when he died, left the island to his friend, Gawsworth. Fleming was greatly amused by Gawsworth's statement that he had never seen the island as he couldn't afford to travel out there, but added: 'I keep up the tradition of the Kingdom of Redonda and hold court once a year with some of my "dukes", who are all literary figures intent on perpetuating the name of Shiel.'

Periodically the romantically minded Gawsworth bestowed Redondan titles on various people. Ian Fleming was made a 'duke' of Redonda 'for services rendered during World War II and for telling the world of the joy of life in small islands'. Among other recipients of Redondan honours were Dirk Bogarde, Rebecca West, J.B. Priestley and Naomi Jacobs, while Diana Dors was made 'Duchess of Redonda' because of her 'services to beauty and charity'.

'A splendid character for a romantic novel' was how Fleming described Gawsworth.[13]

Goldeneye became famous world-wide in November 1956, when Fleming offered Sir Anthony Eden, then Prime Minister, the chance of recuperating in Jamaica after his illness. A large number of journalists swooped on to the island, aiming to stay as close to Goldeneye as they could. They were all eager for copy, but Eden declined to give any interviews.

# 8

# The 'Mercury Empire'

To his coevals here he was the most stimulating of colleagues
and an irreplaceable friend; to younger members of the staff
who came along after him he was and is something of a
legend.[1]

With the war over Fleming urgently needed a career that
would enable him to build up some capital. In mid-1945
this was the main consideration. Yet he was enveloped in three
quite different selves. First, he was loath to let go entirely of the
world of Intelligence that had so fascinated him; secondly, he
hankered after becoming a novelist; and, finally, he saw a com-
promise in returning to a journalistic career.

In the meantime he shook his head sadly as he saw the NID
likely to decline quickly once more, as it had done after the First
World War. During his last days at the Admiralty he tried to
impress upon their senior officers the need for strengthening the
NID rather than let it decline to the old peace-time levels. His
advice was that if through its overseas contacts it gathered commercial and technological intelligence which would help to boost
British industry and sales, the additional expense would more
than pay for itself in the long run. What in fact he was suggesting
was adopting the kind of policy that the Japanese used so effectively after the war, concentrating on gathering intelligence which
would make that nation more prosperous and improve its quality
of life.

A return to journalism would enable him to keep his contacts in
Intelligence by means of his setting up a world-wide project. The

idea which he had shrewdly submitted to Lord Kemsley was to set up a foreign news service for all Kemsley Newspapers, which at that date ranged from *The Sunday Times* and *Daily Sketch* to the *Sunday Graphic*, *Sunday Chronicle*, *Empire News* and the various morning and evening papers in the Kemsley Group from Manchester and Sheffield to Aberdeen, Glasgow, Cardiff and elsewhere. For this appointment Fleming was paid £5,000 a year and, on his insistence, a minimum of two months' paid leave, which he would spend in his Jamaican residence. It was a bold plan, but its expenditure seemed fully justified in view of the large number of newspapers being serviced. No other newspaper proprietor in the whole of the United Kingdom had control of so many journals as Lord Kemsley at that time.

James Gomer Berry, the first Lord Kemsley, was an unusual man to get along with Fleming. A mixture of the prude and the puritan with a sense of his own importance, he was none the less a conscientious journalist who believed that his large chain of newspapers had a great future and that Fleming was the man to provide a world-wide service for the needs of all these papers, individually as well as generally. Fleming had argued that his correspondents would keep just as keen an eye on the kind of story that specially interested Aberdeen or Cardiff as they would for *The Sunday Times* or *Daily Sketch*. He felt that the cost of the service would be amply justified because it could be spread over all the papers. If some of these newspapers had been given a freer hand to be run on more enterprising lines, such expense would have seemed very small indeed. This foreign news service was given the code-name of Mercury, after the Roman messenger god. Incidentally, Fleming's birth sign of Gemini is supposed to be governed by Mercury.

Alas, the tragedy for this ambitious service was that over a period of ten years some of the principal papers ceased publication, while others were taken over. The fault lay not with Fleming but with Lord Kemsley himself: the restraining influence of this press lord frequently prevented many worthwhile journalistic innovations, many of them from Fleming. As well as being foreign manager, Fleming was one of Lord Kemsley's advisers and he constantly urged him to get rid of some of the old fogies on his various papers and replace them with younger men with new ideas. Sometimes he succeeded, but more often he did not.

From the very start of Mercury Fleming sought to ensure that Kemsley Newspapers were given full global coverage. The New York office had four staff members, Paris had five (including one racing correspondent), while there were staff men in Washington, Berlin, Vienna, Tokyo, Jerusalem and the Far East. Within two years an extensive network of string correspondents (i.e. those working on the basis of a retainer plus commissions) was set up all around the world, with special attention being paid to the whole of Africa and the American continent north and south.

The foreign manager (an entirely new post conjured up by Fleming himself and not to be confused with the title of foreign editor) not unnaturally perhaps chose to fill many of the posts in Mercury with those with whom he had been associated in Naval Intelligence and in other branches of the Intelligence services. In each of such appointments, however, the persons selected were also fully qualified journalists and they were not holding such posts merely as a cover for intelligence-gathering. In recent times, particularly after Philby was employed as a Middle East correspondent when he was working for both the British and the USSR, the practice of employing Intelligence personnel as journalists has been frowned upon. The suggestion is that in some way the fact that they are secret agents inhibits them from being good journalists and might prevent them from giving full details of certain news stories. Occasionally, it must be admitted, there could be a clash of loyalties, but on the other hand many such correspondents dating back well into the last century have served their newspapers extremely well and in some cases, in view of their extensive contacts, probably better than many of their colleagues.

Fleming undoubtedly held this latter view and at the same time took the somewhat unusual step of asking his correspondents to supply regularly background information which was confidential and not for publication. These he called 'Sitreps', a term probably borrowed from the wartime Situation Report Centre which was set up 'to collate intelligence received from abroad and to issue daily secret situation reports'. Correspondents' 'Sitreps' went direct to Fleming. (If he happened to be away, they were usually held back until he returned to the office. Once or twice I recall his being telephoned up in Jamaica on some very urgent memorandum of this kind.) Fleming would extract some material from the 'Sitreps' to be circulated to all Kemsley Newspapers editors after it had been duly edited, on the understanding that it was for background information only and not to be quoted directly.

Some of the material obtained from 'Sitreps' was undoubtedly passed on to branches of Intelligence as and when this seemed justified. My own experience as a foreign correspondent based in the then International Zone of Tangier from 1946 to 1949 was that occasionally one could not be sure whether a request from Fleming was intended to produce a story for publication, an answer to an Intelligence problem or information solely for Fleming. I once received a message from him saying 'I want you to meet an amiable rogue named Don Gomez-Beare in the El Minzah Hotel, Tangier, tomorrow at 1800 hours.' No reason for the request was given and, when working for Fleming, one instinctively never queried an instruction or asked for more details: one was supposed to work all that out for oneself. This was partly Fleming's way of testing a correspondent, and, remarkable as it may seem, the method always worked. Luckily, I knew that Gomez-Beare, who was amiable but not a rogue, had worked for Naval Intelligence in the war and that he lived in Gibraltar. Fleming's use of the phrase 'rogue' was intended as a jocular reference to Gomez-Beare's talent for mischievous tactics against the Germans in Spain during the Second World War.

Anthony Cavendish, a former member of MI6 and later a journalist working for the United Press Agency, has stated that 'at the end of the war a number of MI6 agents were sent abroad under the cover of newspaper men. Indeed, the Kemsley Press allowed many of their foreign correspondents to cooperate with MI6 and even took on MI6 operatives as foreign correspondents. However, this practice stopped when Kemsley's disappeared'.[2]

This last sentence refers both to the taking over of Kemsley Newspapers by the late Lord Thomson of Fleet and the subsequent departure of Fleming from their ranks. Among Fleming's early recruits as foreign correspondents for the Mercury network were such people as Antony Terry, Stephen Coulter, Ian Colvin, Cedric Salter, Edward Howe and Keith Butler. Terry, who received the Military Cross for taking part in the St Nazaire Combined Operations raid while serving in Army Intelligence in the war, was taken prisoner by the Germans. On his release he was attached to the Interrogation Section of the War Office. As Mercury correspondent in Vienna he continued with part-time Intelligence service. Coulter, who had been in the Navy, had served as a staff officer for SHAPE Intelligence in France and Scandinavia. He became correspondent in Paris. Colvin, largely on his own initiative, had poured out intelligence to the British authorities as Central European correspondent for the *News Chronicle* in the years immediately before the war. While serving in the Royal Marines from 1941 to 1945 he was linked to the Political Warfare Executive and the SOE. Fleming appointed him as correspondent in Germany, where he soon made a name for himself as one of the best-informed commentators of the day.

Cedric Salter was of course a contact of Fleming's regarding Admiral Canaris, as has already been noted. He had made a name for himself as a reporter on the Spanish Civil War and later as a war correspondent in the Middle East and Far East. He was based in Barcelona for Mercury. Edward Howe had been Reuters correspondent in Vienna and Budapest prior to 1939 and in the war joined the British Army for special service in the Balkans. He parachuted into Yugoslavia and for his work with the Partisans was awarded the MBE. Fleming appointed him to Istanbul.

Kemsley's foreign manager also remembered former colleagues in the NID and the Admiralty. Lt-Commander William Todd, RNVR, who had been head of Thomas Cook & Sons Berkeley Street office pre-war and was an expert on Egypt, was put in charge of travel arrangements in the Mercury Foreign Department. While in the NID he had been chief of the Scandinavian section, his principal role being to liaise with the Swedish naval attaché, Count Oxenstjerna. John Drummond, another Admiralty officer and previously a Press Association reporter, was appointed to New York. Yet another correspondent with associations with the world of Intelligence was Leslie Smith in Hong Kong. He had been covering events in the Far East since the early 1930s and had later served with the British Intelligence service in China.

Fleming retained a liking for Scots to work for him. Quite apart from some Scottish correspondents overseas, at one time he had no fewer than five Scots, including myself, working for him in the London office of Mercury. Three of these were also Ians, though each spelt differently – Iain Lang, Ion Seton Munro and Ian Forsyth Munro.

It is not generally known that Fleming's first book was not *Casino Royale*. It was in fact a pocket-size but detailed and constructive foreign correspondents' guide-book. This was not known outside the Foreign Department of Kemsley Newspapers: it was issued under the curt title of *Mercury Reference Book* for Mercury staff at home and overseas. From my own experience as a string correspondent covering Morocco, Algeria, Tunisia, Libya and as far south as French Equatorial Africa, I can confirm that it was invaluable. I would go further and say that it was worth a small fortune to any string correspondent, for it pointed out the scope for a wide variety of stories and features. Any correspondent who could not earn a living from it deserved to be sacked.

A foreign stringer's life is not the choice many journalists would make. It can on occasions impose a severe mental strain, as it is essential to be looking ahead the whole time with an eye to what sort of commissions one is going to make over and above one's retainer. It is a life that calls for a spirit of adventure and a fairly keen and even grim sense of humour. Fleming's book was just the stimulus one needed. He urged one 'to get to know what the local news agency men filed and whether they filed promptly'. Such knowledge enabled a correspondent to know how and when to beat the agencies' correspondents. Where Fleming's book helped correspondents most, however, was in stressing that there was scope for stories not in just one paper but in nearly a score of journals, daily, evening, Sunday and even provincial weekly papers. 'When you travel around find out whether there are any people worth a story who hail from Aberdeen, Glasgow, Manchester, Sheffield, Cardiff, etc. living in the area. If so, get a story out of them.' To cite some typical examples of how this advice proved invaluable, I recall discovering in Marrakesh a Scottish golf professional to the pasha of that city, while in Casablanca I met a Welsh woman from Caerphilly whose wartime adventures made even *The Thirty-Nine Steps* seem dull. Even in Tripoli I came across the 2nd Battalion of the Cheshire Regiment, which resulted in a lengthy article for the *Macclesfield Times*.

In his guide-book Fleming urged correspondents all over the world to bear in mind the various industries in those areas where Kemsley had provincial papers – steel in the Sheffield district, for example. The object was to watch out for any story that might usefully touch on any of those industries, or in some cases point to a market for their products. If some controversy loomed large in Britain, Fleming would want to know how a similar problem would be tackled overseas. When the National Health Service was founded, Fleming circulated various carefully chosen foreign correspondents to find out which was the best health service in the world. This resulted in a lengthy feature on New Zealand's NHS.

This guide-book also made suggestions as to how Mercury's team should look out for subjects for feature-length articles as well as straight news. Each month both staffmen and stringers were urged to produce a feature article on their particular area, giving it some topicality or newsworthy theme. Equally, correspondents were urged to contribute regularly short, gossipy stories ranging from items for the 'Atticus' column of *The Sunday Times* to the *Daily Sketch*'s 'Inside Information' feature and 'Window on the World', which appeared regularly in most of the provincial papers. That the Mercury team was an undoubted success may be gleaned from the statistics compiled of their published material. Officially, 'in 1946 the total wordage of Mercury correspondents published in Kemsley Newspapers was about two and a half million. Three years later it had risen to nearly four million'.[3]

Surprisingly, *The Sunday Times*, which should have gone all out to absorb the best of Mercury's material, was, in the late 1940s at least, much less interested than other Kemsley Newspapers. This was partly because not only did the paper then lack a foreign editor, but it had an aged editor in W.W. Hadley, who never travelled abroad and spent every holiday in Droitwich. He had the attitude towards stories from overseas that 'It's not in the news, so forget it.' Fleming's attitude was the reverse: 'Nobody's heard of this before, so make sure you put it in the news.' His other great stimulant for his correspondents was that 'life has got to be fun'. His final comment to me when eventually he gave up his news-paper work was 'It was all great fun while it lasted.'

'We British have to be exhibitionists,' he said. 'It is a very healthy thing for us to be exhibitionists. This is a Nordic country. People of the North ought to get wild occasionally. People of the South are wild all the time out of *joie de vivre*. But it's precisely because the Briton lacks *joie de vivre* that he wants to put on a paper hat occasionally and pretend he has *joie de vivre*. I think it's an excellent way of releasing bottled-up feelings. What often gets overlooked is that the Nordic people have much more depth of feeling than the Mediterranean ones. That's why you get much more psychosomatic troubles in the North. You very seldom find a psychologically deranged Italian, whereas if you go to Sweden you find the place practically crawling with them.'

This was the down-to-earth practicality which both controlled and inspired his romanticism. He also possessed a certain amount of what those of us who had been in the Navy called 'black humour'. It was a rather special kind of naval humour and not all Navy men appreciated it.

Fleming's temperament was essentially romantic and he be-lieved in introducing something of this spirit into everyday work. He even adopted these tactics at his morning conferences at Kemsley House, especially when spirits were low on account of the closure of some paper or some lesser upset. It was then he would make a joke and insist that efficiency would always be impaired 'unless work is made fun'. The introduction of naval jargon in a newspaper office made him feel that running a depart-ment such as Mercury had the same kind of excitement as con-ducting a war. Thus a message to a correspondent was 'a signal' and for a cabled rebuke he used the naval 'Mark One Bottle' (a term designating a severe ticking-off, usually by a senior officer).

It was Fleming who insisted that his correspondents be given bylines. It took some tactful persuasion on his part to convince Lord Kemsley on this question, since hitherto naming a corre-spondent when printing his story had been regarded as somewhat vulgar. Fleming's view was that this was a morale-booster for a correspondent far distant from his office. Sometimes he ordered a correspondent to change his name if he did not like it. His view was that, generally speaking, all foreign correspondents should have British-sounding names. Mario Modiano in Athens became Michael Manning, Mozandi in Teheran became Mostyn, while Geoffrey Bocca in New York one day received a terse cable from Fleming saying: ALLEZ BOCCA AVE BARKER.

Once, however, Fleming had this trick played back on him. When Anthony Berry, Lord Kemsley's youngest son, was editing the *Sunday Chronicle*, a story came in from the Gibraltar correspondent on a security issue and a request that his byline should not be used. This occurred shortly after Fleming had his first novel published. 'We must have some byline,' said Anthony Berry. 'Why not James Bond, Gibraltar?' This byline was duly used.

Fleming was particularly good at covering up for a correspondent who had received important confidential information. When I was a correspondent in Tangier I was given the story of a purge of the CIA following leakages of highly confidential information and evidence of communist infiltration into key positions. My informant was a US diplomat and he stressed that on no account must the story be traced to him. I explained the situation to Mercury in London, stressing that my name and a Tangier dateline must not be used with the story. Back came a cable from Fleming saying: YOUR UNISTATES PURGE HIT FIVE EVENINGS YESTERDAY STOP DATELINE BALTIMORE.

In the early days after the war newsprint shortage and small papers created space problems for all forms of news. Because of this some of the senior executives of Kemsley Newspapers who were jealous of Fleming argued that his foreign service was a gross extravagance. In fact, had *The Sunday Times* then used more foreign news, as *The Observer* was doing, nobody could have complained because all the other papers gave Mercury stories an excellent show. As to the gradual disappearance of newspapers such as the other Sunday papers and eventually the *Daily Sketch*, that wasn't Fleming's fault. Certainly he splashed out on congratulatory cables to foreign correspondents when their stories were used, but he did so to boost morale and make the man in a distant place feel he was appreciated. Yet all Fleming's Scottish instincts of financial prudence came to bear when it came to wasting time on the telephone. When I was back in London as Commonwealth Editor in the 1950s he was frequently urging me to 'boom so-and-so off the telephone': 'Don't let him chatter to secretaries before he gets through to you.' 'Remind him that the teleprinter can often save money.'

Nevertheless Fleming's envious critics in the hierarchy sought to impose their will when the pound was devalued in 1949 by insisting that he maintained too large an administrative staff in London. Fleming responded rather cleverly by persuading Lord Kemsley to make Iain Lang, the editor of the *Sunday Graphic*, not only deputy foreign manager but foreign editor of *The Sunday Times* as well, this being the first time that paper had had a foreign editor. Fleming was also able to point out that, as far as making economies was concerned, he had always insisted on all stories and articles which were not instant news material being sent by airmail.[4]

Fleming had visited Tangier during the war in connection with his NID duties and he had been astonished at the concentration of the world's intelligence services in what was then still an international zone. At the end of the war many of the various agents and spies of all nationalities found themselves faced with the prospect of either dwindling work or no work at all. Some of them responded by turning themselves into free-lance agents, eager to sell their stories to a journalist anxious to listen. When he appointed me to base myself in Tangier, but at the same time to cover all Morocco, Algeria, Tunisia, Libya, Nigeria and French West Africa, arranging personal contacts in all these areas, he also had in mind his own idea of a personal secret service. Thus he was very keen to get the kind of story such as the one for which he gave a Baltimore dateline. He looked on Tangier as a main source for obtaining world-wide intelligence quite apart from newspaper stories.

At that time he was very interested in setting up an English daily or weekly newspaper in Tangier which would circulate in Spain and Portugal as well as the whole of North Africa. Tangier then had a small weekly newspaper, the *Tangier Gazette*, containing local news: it was owned by the family of the Marquess of Bute whose commercial interests in the area were considerable. One day I had a letter from Fleming which stated: 'Regarding the *Tangier Gazette*, it seems to me that if the Butes wind it up, we could take over the nuts and bolts and run it as the *Mediterranean Times*. If we serialised your book [I was then thinking of writing a book entitled *Spy Society* about the international spy city of Tangier], we might get off to a flying start as the cloakies in Gibraltar would buy up so many copies to send home to their chiefs. . . . Please keep an eye open on any possibilities.'[5]

Fleming had linked up with a small group of friends, including Gomez-Beare and Commander Alan Hillgarth (formerly the senior naval attaché in Madrid), who had shown an interest in acquiring or creating an English language newspaper based in Tangier. This project fell through, but the persistent Fleming persuaded Dennis Berry, another of Lord Kemsley's sons, to fly out to Tangier to investigate further. As a result, some time later I was brought back to London to help produce a dummy for the *Mediterranean Times*. The plan was eventually turned down by the Kemsley board of directors.

I recall receiving one cable from Fleming which caused the Eastern Telegraph Company staff in Tangier to regard me with some suspicious glances. It said: THANKS YOUR RUSSIAN SKULL-DUGGERY OUTSIDE CURTAIN. It referred to a story of mine about Soviet espionage in Algeria, but I'm sure the ETC people thought I had personally been indulging in some mischief on behalf of the USSR.

Fleming tried hard to get some worthwhile news out of Moscow when Cyril Ray, a former writer on the *Manchester Guardian*, was appointed correspondent there. It was a frustrating time for Ray whose movements were severely restricted under the Stalinist regime. As is recorded in the history of *The Sunday Times*, Ray was prevented 'from writing anything but descriptive and diminutive essays on Moscow life. An elaborate fiction was maintained that there *was* no censorship. Correspondents were graciously accorded "literary guidance". He [Ray] sometimes asked to see the censor, to argue a point. "But there is no censor, Mr Ray"'.

One of Fleming's foremost protégés was Oscar Henry Brandon, formerly known as Oscar Brandeis, a Czech émigré. He became an outstanding correspondent in Washington and his dispatches attracted attention world-wide, thanks to the syndication of Mercury's news service. In Brandon's appointments questionnaire he put the name of Ian Fleming as his next of kin. No relationship, of course, but it suggests once again how Fleming was some kind of father to us all. Long after Fleming's death the Soviet newspaper *Izvestia* accused Brandon of being an agent of British Intelligence.[6]

When Mercury was at its peak, Fleming had got together a team of eighty-eight foreign correspondents covering every area of the globe from Hollywood to Fiji. In addition, Fleming's careful development of the syndication of his news service greatly enhanced the effectiveness of Mercury. The news and features service was taken by newspapers in Australia, Canada and South Africa as well as NANA, the North American Newspaper Alliance, a consortium of newspapers working together to acquire rights they could not afford separately. This was an organization set up by two old friends of Fleming's, Ivar Bryce and Ernest Cuneo, and Fleming himself became European vice-president of NANA. Fleming asked me to provide for NANA – quite distinctly from anything I wrote for Kemsley Newspapers – a weekly feature to be called 'International Inside Information'.

Ernest Cuneo's family had been responsible for starting the Cuneo Press in Chicago. After leaving Columbia University Cuneo had become a lawyer and during the war he was closely linked to the British Intelligence set-up in New York as well as the American OSS. He was a vigilant and enterprising operator with NANA and was constantly urging Fleming to produce exciting series of articles with big names attached to them. One such attempt Fleming made was to try to persuade Major-General Sir Colin Gubbins to write a popular history of the SOE. In a letter addressed to 'Dear Colin' on 7 July 1949, he stressed that 'you are the only person who could do this and who would also have the confidence of the Ministry of Defence as far as security matters were concerned'.[7] On this occasion Fleming was not successful and it was not until 1966 that an official history of the SOE by M.R.D. Foote was published,[8] while Gubbins's own book, *The Fourth Dimension of Warfare* did not appear until 1968.

Time after time Fleming forcefully stood up for his foreign correspondents when some story of theirs was disputed by the authorities. On one occasion when I was stationed in Tangier false information was received that there was a Jewish plot to blow up the British Consulate-General in Tangier. As a result one of HM frigates was sent over to Tangier from Gibraltar with armed troops on what turned out to be a false errand. Yet when I filed the story for *The Sunday Times*, in which it was duly printed, there were loud denials from the British Consul-General in Tangier, the Foreign Office and the Admiralty as well as the Ministry of Defence. Fortunately Fleming backed me up against all such attempts to suppress my story.[9]

A first-class scoop was organized by Fleming when he requested Richard Hughes, Mercury's chief Far East correspondent, to return to London on his biennial leave via Moscow. After spending some time in Moscow, Hughes managed to get the first interview with the two missing British diplomats, Maclean and Burgess.

Hughes ('Dikko', as Fleming called him) had always been one of the most highly efficient of Mercury correspondents and was a lively and amusing character. It is a tribute to his attractive personality that both Fleming and John Le Carré used him as a model for characters in their books. 'To know Dick,' wrote Le Carré after Hughes's death in the 1980s, 'was to have a living history book of modern South-East Asia at your finger-tips; to enjoy his trust was to enter an exotic masonry of devoted friends all over the region from Macao to Korea.' Fleming and he had carefully planned the Moscow stop-off with the aim of persuading the Russians to let Burgess and Maclean talk. At the same time Fleming had produced his own ploy for bringing off this scoop: he fed Hughes with a certain amount of information to feed in turn to the Russians (nothing in any way damaging to British interests, of course) and suggested that Hughes should convey to Khrushchev and Bulganin, who were shortly to visit Britain, that if they could produce the two diplomats beforehand, it would make for better relations when they arrived in London.

There was a hush-hush memorandum to Hughes from Fleming on this subject, on which Hughes acted with speed and imagination. He managed to obtain a personal interview with Molotov at which he handed him a memorandum of his own which was marked: 'To be given to President Bulganin and Mr Khrushchev'. In this memorandum Hughes stressed that it was in their interests that they should reveal that the two men were alive and that failure to do so would possibly ruin their visit to Britain. As a result, though Hughes did not get a personal interview with Burgess and Maclean, he met them and received their joint statements.

Hughes was also used by Fleming for what was generally known as China-watching. In his base at Hong Kong, to which he moved after leaving Tokyo, Hughes described what he called 'information from and about China droppeth like the heavy rain from heaven upon the Hong Kong watcher beneath, but flooding and often confusing, rather than blessing, him that takes'.[10] But Hughes also made occasional trips into communist China, notably in 1956 when he returned to Shanghai which he had not seen for some years. A few years before, when Fleming was in the United States on a brief visit and I was deputizing for him in London, Iain Lang, who was then simply foreign editor of *The Sunday Times* and no longer deputy foreign manager of Mercury, came into my office and announced with a somewhat enigmatic smile on his face: 'I have been into Fleming's office and taken the whole of his file on Dick Hughes. I think the chairman [Lord Kemsley] will be somewhat displeased with the news that Dick is being used for *other purposes*', underlining the last two words with an ironic tone in his voice.

Lang, who was a discreet left-winger while still managing to win Lord Kemsley's respect, was an admirer of Mao Tse-tung and strongly disapproved of any kind of China-watching other than the strictly journalistic. He seemed to be suggesting that Fleming's confidential files concerning Hughes revealed that our man in Hong Kong was in some way gathering intelligence for an organization other than Kemsley Newspapers. I telephoned Fleming in New York and warned him of what had happened. 'You have your own files on Dikko,' he said. 'Make sure that they are kept out of sight until I get back.'

When Commonwealth editor of Mercury I was in frequent touch with the late Arthur Morley Richards, our chief Kemsley correspondent in Australia. It was about this time that British football pools firms started introducing Australian soccer matches into their coupons. Nobody in Britain knew anything about Australian soccer form and I was asked by the Sports Department of Kemsley Newspapers to try to find somebody who could do forecasts to publish in the group papers. Richards reported back that as British-style soccer then aroused relatively little interest in Australia, there were no established newspapers forecasters in the country, as was the case in Britain. To cope with such a demand would mean obtaining somewhat haphazard and unprofessional forecasts from about half a dozen people in different areas of Australia. 'It will be very much hit and miss, I'm afraid,' wrote Richards, who had for a brief period been deputy foreign manager of Mercury in London. 'Curiously enough, I'm told by my stringer in Canberra that, though he knows nothing about soccer himself, the best informed judge of local soccer there is none other than one Vladimir Petrov, of the Soviet Embassy. How about trying to line him up?'

Richards was of course joking when he made this suggestion, as he can hardly have expected to sign up a Soviet official. But naturally I informed Fleming and he was almost immediately hugely interested in the idea. He took the view that however improbable it might seem to sign him up, just to see what happened we should offer him a small retainer to give us match forecasts. 'We can't lose either way' was Fleming's comment. 'It's certainly worth a try, if only to learn more about the Russians. After all Petrov is more a spy than a diplomat. That much I have already ascertained. It's always just possible that we might pull off a real scoop by persuading him to defect to our side.'

Here was Fleming's wartime brain ticking over again. He was absolutely right, of course: had we been able to make such approaches a few weeks earlier, we could have had a major scoop. But before we could take the matter further, the news of Petrov's defection broke. Australia's Security Service had decided some time before that Petrov was worth watching in case he could be lured into defecting. His habit of watching local soccer matches in the Canberra area had been noted and, unknown to him, two Australian security men had shadowed him at these matches and reported back to their chief that in an unguarded moment Petrov had said to another spectator: 'This is a splendid game. I am glad you have taken it up. I should be quite happy to stay for ever in your lovely country.'

However, having exclusively got the story of Petrov's interest in soccer, we were able to exploit it fully when news of his defection broke. Our detailed story was headed 'So Petrov the spy found his goal'. Certainly his defection gave not only Australia but Britain a remarkable insight into Soviet espionage tactics. He named more than six hundred Soviet agents around the world. Petrov died in Melbourne, aged eighty-four, in 1991.

Yet the memories of most who worked for Mercury during these immediate and exciting post-war years are of the way in which Fleming always found time to go far beyond any normal practices for an employer in looking after his staff and stringers. If some correspondent desperately needed to return to the United Kingdom permanently for domestic or other serious reasons, the foreign manager not only sympathized but did his utmost to find him a job in London. Or, if not London, then in Manchester or Glasgow. 'I was particularly glad to see your article in the *Spectator* last week,' he wrote to me in Tangier on one occasion. 'This is just the sort of dispatch which should have been published in the *Sunday Times* if they were not so desperately short of space and so very much concerned with domestic politics here.' Most other executive journalists in positions similar to that of Fleming would have commented: 'What is the meaning of the article you wrote for the *Spectator* last week, and why was it not sent to *The Sunday Times*?' Fleming went far beyond this. In that very same letter he added: 'Did you have any success with *The Economist* or with any other of my suggestions such as *Holiday*, the new American magazine?'

Other correspondents found him just as helpful. Antony Terry, for many years one of Mercury's most valuable correspondents in Vienna, Berlin, Bonn and Paris, confirms this. 'He was one of the most generous-hearted people I have ever met. From the moment I joined Kemsley and went out to Vienna, all through the subsequent years, he took a warm and understanding interest in one's work and one's personal affairs, always ready to offer advice and assistance, often unasked,' Terry wrote in a letter to me.

Some of Fleming's letters to Terry indicate his keen appreciation of correspondents' problems. In 1949 he wrote: 'Try not to get too stuck in press camps and visit theatres and cinemas as much as you can. I shall never mind being beaten on spot news, if I feel that you are devoting your time to becoming really acquainted with all aspects of your fascinating and dangerous territory and its psychosis-ridden inhabitants.' That letter[11] was sent when Terry was stationed at the British Press Camp in Dusseldorf.

In 1949, the effect on the foreign service of the pound's devaluation was considerable, especially in the way it increased costs of correspondents in Germany. Fleming took it upon himself to make representations to the Foreign Office that something ought to be done about this. He wrote in forthright style to Sir Ivone Kirkpatrick, Permanent Under-Secretary at the German Section of the Foreign Office, saying: 'We have ninety correspondents round the world and the most expensive to maintain, exclusive of salary, is our representative in Washington at some £4,500 a year. To have to pay nearly double that sum for our representative in Germany will, I fear, make this appointment laughably uneconomical.' Fleming took the view that the obvious answer to this question was to have a diplomatic mark rate for the benefit of Control Commission employees in Germany and duly accredited correspondents. Later be wrote to Terry to say that 'it is clear that the Foreign Office are getting very busy as a result of my broadside'.[12]

Fleming was far from being just a 'desk-man'. He once wrote to Terry saying: 'I wonder if you could keep your eyes open for a suitable assignment of the sort of adventurous type which has become my speciality. . . . I wonder if there is anything in that story of the German who claims to have discovered Atlantis under the sea off Heligoland?'[13]

Auberon Waugh in a *Sunday Telegraph* review once described Fleming as 'a total disaster' and 'selfish and mean'. At the same time he suggested that some of Ian's friends might write in about his more positive qualities. The invitation was taken up by Philip Brownrigg, who replied in a letter which said:

When I was working for him [Ian] at Kemsley Newspapers, I
had my last year as a Territorial soldier. At our summer camp,
on the final working day, the battalion I commanded was
involved in a tragic accident, when shells from a supporting
battery landed in the middle of my leading company, killing one
man and wounding others. As soon as I got home Ian
telephoned to say that he was driving down to the country to
see me. When he arrived, he said that I must not come back to
the office until I had recovered from the shock and had done
what I could to help those really affected. He then told me that
he had arranged for his cottage at St. Margaret's Bay to be
ready for my wife and me for a couple of weeks' rest. Just
before he left he wrote a substantial cheque for the fund we had
started in aid of those who had suffered in the accident. 'Selfish
and mean'? He was a marvellous boss and friend, intensely loyal
to his staff, always ready to defend and help them. I owe him
more than I can ever say.[14]

# 9

## *Vesper Lynd*

'I was born in the evening, on a very stormy evening
according to my parents. Apparently they wanted to remember it.'[1]

'O'ne of the most eligible bachelors in London' was how
some of Fleming's friends described him in the early
days after the war. Tall, handsome, with a marked touch of
panache, he had always been popular with women, including
those who worked for him. Yet despite the fact that all his life he
had revelled in feminine company, he remained basically a natural
bachelor, always wary of becoming entangled with one woman.

Alan Schneider, who had become a confidant of Fleming in
London during the war, said of him: 'He never really cared too
much about the English girls – he said they smelled because they
didn't bathe enough and they didn't know the first thing about
making love. . . . He told me that he never wanted to get married. Women were fine to make love to, but you didn't have to
marry them.'[2]

Fleming could not stand undue adoration and many women not
only adored him but frequently advertised the fact. There is a clue
to this in Fleming's first novel, *Casino Royale*, in which James
Bond comments: 'Women were for recreation. On a job, they got
in the way and fogged things up with sex and hurt feelings and all
the emotional baggage they carried around. One had to look out
for them and take care of them.'

Schneider says that 'he seemed to be ruthless about women
. . . . He got bored with them fast'.[3] Yet if one studies the whole
of the quotation from *Casino Royale*, one can detect a desire by

139

Fleming via Bond to be honest about himself with women and not to pretend to be other than what he was, while at the same time realizing that, though it could be tiresome and even irksome, one had to 'take care of them'.

Those who knew Fleming closely, thought that he dreaded the idea of marriage and felt it would be an impediment to his career and his love of frequent adventure. Yet by the late 1940s he had considerable problems in his love life, despite his freedom as a bachelor. There had been one or two tragedies as well: he had lost contact with Vanessa, his German girl-friend, and it irked him that he could get no news of her. There had also been a dispatch rider for the NID of whom he had been quite fond. She had been killed in the Blitz. From all accounts, her death had saddened him quite deeply. He had enjoyed her company and commented afterwards: 'Alas, she was far too good for me – too good to be true.' What he enjoyed most of all were women with whom he could share enjoyable recreations with no strings attached. This particularly applied to women in Jamaica with whom he could go underwater exploring. However, the real and vital amatory problems for Fleming in this period concerned two totally different women in his life: Anne, Lady Rothermere, and Christine Granville.

Apart from all the imbroglios relating to Anne, Fleming had a problem with his employer, the late Lord Kemsley. Gomer Kemsley came from a somewhat rigid Welsh religious background and placed great emphasis on the sanctity of family life. He greatly disliked divorce, especially when it involved members of his own staff. He also took the view that he, his family and his employees should not in any way embarrass or clash with rival newspaper tycoons and their families. A divorce involving Fleming, his foreign manager, threatened to do just this. Yet Fleming never gave any impression that any of this worried him, though in the long run it probably cost him the chance of a directorship of Kemsley Newspapers. He was on especially good terms with Lord Kemsley's second wife, Edith, whose background was in distinct contrast to that of her husband. She came from a French-Mauritian family, which may have made for a more broad-minded approach on her part to Fleming's quandary.

Yet what is most fascinating about Fleming's life at this time is that, even while he pondered on whether or not to marry Anne, he had another woman in his life. She was everything that Anne was not. She was at once sexually attractive, unlike Anne, whose charms derived from her personality and conversational talents. Ian's new-found friend was highly intelligent, quick-witted, amusing, astonishingly brave and always in quest of adventure. Nobody else could quite come up to the ideal of a James Bond heroine, which ultimately was exactly what she became. Moreover she had carried out true-life feats of daring espionage in an official capacity. 'I see exactly what you mean about Christine,' Fleming wrote in a letter to one of his correspondents, Edward Howe. 'She literally shines with all the qualities and splendours of a fictitious character. How rarely one finds such types.'[4]

The daughter of Count Jerzy Skarbek, who had married Stephanie Goldfeder, daughter of a Polish-Jewish banker, she was christened Krystina following her birth in May 1915. Educated at a convent school, where she was noted for frequent misbehaviour, she was married at the age of eighteen to Charles Getlich. The marriage soon broke up and in 1938 she married again, this time to George (Jerzy) Gizychi at the Evangelical Reform Church in Warsaw. Gizychi took Christine to Kenya in 1939 and soon afterwards their marriage began to break up.

Somehow she had suddenly become enamoured with Britain and all she felt it stood for. She even imagined herself becoming a secret agent for the British and, with this in mind, she and George went to London, contacted the Foreign Office and offered to go to Bucharest to collect intelligence. In support of such offers she said: 'I don't think I've ever felt what is called fear.' Certainly she lived up to this personal claim of hers when she went to Budapest, making a series of hazardous journeys to rescue patriots from the Gestapo. Her close colleague and loyal friend in Budapest was Andrezej Kowerski, later known as Major Andrew Kennedy, another valiant supporter of the Allied cause. Together they helped a number of people to join the various Resistance movements which were then being set up.

On one occasion the Hungarian police and the Gestapo were so baffled by her that she managed to slip into the bathroom and flush an incriminating piece of paper down the lavatory. Eventually she managed to escape from further investigations by going to Cairo in 1942. Here she was given a small retainer by the SOE. Then in 1944 she was dropped into southern France as an SOE agent to work with the Resistance. The man who asked for her to be sent took the view that a woman would be less conspicuous than a man in such underground work. He was Francis Cammaerts, who at that time controlled an area which extended from Lyon to the Swiss border. Christine arrived by parachute, saying that 'I drop real well, *comme un torchon*, because I'm exactly like a wet dishcloth.'[5]

Officially attached to the WAAF service, Christine operated under SOE instructions with the code-name of 'Pauline'. The circuit in which she worked was named 'Jockey', and in his book *SOE in France* M.R.D. Foote records that Christine was parachuted into France on 6/7 July 1944. He goes on to say that when at last the Gestapo arrested Cammaerts at a road control, 'his new courier, the Polish Christine Granville, by a combination of steady nerve, feminine cunning and sheer brass persuaded his captors that the Americans' arrival was imminent, and secured the party's release three hours before they were due to have been shot'.

Xan Fielding, who was with Cammaerts at the time, later recorded: 'Christine arrived at Digne prison and passed herself off as Cammaerts' wife, as well as claiming to be a niece of General Montgomery. . . . As a result Cammaerts and I were led out of prison. Believing ourselves about to be taken away to be shot, we were astounded when we found Christine was waiting for us with a car.'[6]

At the end of the war Christine was awarded the George Medal in addition to the OBE. But despite this, she felt she had been badly let down by the British after the war, when, with no funds of her own (her second marriage had ended by this time), she was demobilized in May 1945, with a gratuity of a mere £100 and no promise of a job. That she had been treated in a mean fashion was a view shared by all her friends. SOE officials, who had promised her some form of security, made no effort to help her. She obtained British nationality and took up the name of Granville after it had been suggested to her by Kate O'Reilly, the daughter of Sir Owen O'Reilly, formerly British Ambassador in Budapest. She chose this name because it had both British and French associations.

Christine had great difficulty in obtaining a worthwhile job. In 1947 she went to Cairo where she met an old friend, Edward Howe, the Kemsley Newspapers correspondent, who was visiting the Egyptian capital from his base in Istanbul. Howe told me: 'As a long shot I gave her Fleming's address, as I felt sure he would be interested in her – as a fascinating personality certainly and maybe as a correspondent somewhere or other.'

Fleming was interested and he arranged to meet Christine for the first time at Bertorelli's restaurant in Charlotte Street. I learned this much one day when Fleming asked me to let him have clippings from the office library of any newspaper stories about Christine Granville and various people with whom she had been on close terms. I recall that Fleming was particularly amused when I announced that Christine was reported to have won a 'Miss Poland' beauty contest at the age of eighteen. I recall the lunch-date because shortly before he left the office for this appointment Fleming asked me to look up some other details about Granville and to telephone him at Bertorelli's during the lunch-hour.

Ian and Christine continued to meet from time to time, though opportunities to do so were few and far between because Christine had become a stewardess on a passenger ship. Years afterwards one of Christine's Polish friends, Olga Bialoguski, told me that Christine was almost obsessively secretive. She would make up a story on the spur of the moment to cover her tracks. Possibly this was because of her wartime work and it had given her the habit. She suddenly found that there were few people she could trust. This even applied to some members of the Polish Women's Association in London. She certainly kept her meetings with Fleming very much of a secret. If she wanted to meet him, she would get me to put through a message to him, using the name of some male and Olga was to ask Fleming or his secretary for a time to meet Mr X, or whatever the name was. It was understood by him that this was a signal for him to meet Christine. Olga never quite knew why she did this, whether it was somehow to impress

Fleming with her secretive nature, or whether the plan was Fleming's. Olga said she must have been one of the very few of Christine's friends, perhaps the only woman friend, who shared this secret. They usually met at some small hotel or restaurant far away from the usual haunts of either of them.

I asked if they were lovers.

'Christine was not one to talk about the men in her life,' Olga Bialoguski replied. 'For a while I thought this relationship with Fleming must be tied up with some kind of undercover intelligence work. After all, that made sense: she had been in the Resistance and he had been in Naval Intelligence. But as time went on I became convinced it was more than that. Once she told me that Fleming had introduced her to a hotel named the Granville somewhere in the region of Dover, and she was very amused by that.'

This brought back memories of *Moonraker* (1955). Fleming had sited somewhere in the region of St Margaret's Bay and Kingsdown the Moonraker missile built by the villain, Hugo Drax. Bond took the heroine of *Moonraker*, Gala Brand, for a walk along the beach in that area after Drax had tried to kill them with an arranged cliff fall. 'Come on,' he said, 'it's nearly six o'clock. The tide's coming in fast, but we can get to St Margaret's before it catches us. We'll clean up at the Granville there and have a drink and some food.'

The Granville Hotel, about to be pulled down at the time of writing, was patronized by both Fleming and Noël Coward. To introduce Christine to a hotel actually named after her would be just the kind of joke Fleming would enjoy.

'Can you recall anything else about Fleming and Christine?' I asked Olga.

'Once they spent a weekend together at Dieppe and after that I do recall that Christine did let the curtain of secrecy drop for a few moments. She told me that for almost the first time since the war she had actually enjoyed "a few magical hours" – yes, that was her exact phrase – with someone it was a delight to be with. You can interpret that as you like. One did not ask Christine for details.'

The year 1952 was a memorable one for Fleming, as almost everything good and bad seemed to happen to him throughout that period. The Rothermeres had obtained their divorce and there was now nothing to prevent Fleming from marrying Anne. It still seemed as though he had considerable doubts about the wisdom of such a union, as two statements by Fleming himself show only too clearly. Some years later he described how and when he started to write thrillers in January 1952: 'After being a bachelor for forty-four years I was on the edge of marrying and the prospect was so horrifying that I was in urgent need of some activity to take my mind off it. . . . I have a puritanical dislike of idleness and a natural love of action. I decided to write a book.'[7]

This book was of course *Casino Royale*. While putting the finishing touches to this work he wrote to Hugo and Virginia Charteris, Anne's brother and his wife, saying: 'We [i.e. Anne and himself] are, of course, totally unsuited – both Gemini. I'm a non-communicator, a symmetrist of a bilious and melancholy temperament, only interested in tomorrow. Anne is a sanguine anarchist/traditionalist. So china will fly and there will be rage and tears. But I think we are both optimistic, and I shall never hurt her except with a slipper.'[8]

Here is evidence of at least a casual acquaintance with astrology on the part of Fleming. I asked Olga Bialoguski if she had heard any mention of astrology concerning Ian and Christine, to which she replied: 'Christine was born under the sign of Taurus and she made a point of asking people what their signs of the zodiac were. I asked her what Fleming was, but I cannot remember what she said now. All I do recall is that she said he was always telling her that his sign of the zodiac meant he was at least two different people, maybe even three.'

Two quotations are worth considering in relation to this comment by Olga Bialoguski. William Plomer in his memorial address to Fleming said: 'I have heard it said that there were several different Ians, and that he kept different parts of his life quite separate. If this is true, it is one more proof that the popular image of him is far too crude and flat.' The second quotation comes from Liz Greene, a practising psychologist and astrologist. Referring to male Geminis she writes: 'There are two of him. . . .

One moment the world is shining and full of light, the next it's dark and imprisoning. It's one of the reasons why Geminis are so good at reporting and writing and dealing with the public. They're acutely sensitive to both faces of life and are usually well-stocked with both idealism and cynicism. They see both and are both.'[9] Regardless of anything that astrologers may say, both these assessments apply accurately to the character of Ian Fleming.

The marriage of Ian and Anne was probably hastened by the fact that Anne was expecting a child by Fleming. Nuptials were conducted at a civil ceremony at Port Maria, Jamaica, by special licence from the then Governor, Sir Hugh Foot. Noël Coward and his secretary Cole Leslie were witnesses and guests afterwards at a small reception at Goldeneye. The menu for the wedding breakfast, or *breykinge* as it is called in Jamaica, consisted of turtle caught by Fleming, which Coward described as exactly like chewing an old Dunlop tyre, and black crab, which he compared to cigarette ash. In the Associated Press report of the marriage Fleming was described as 'a London journalist'. In view of this it is not surprising that he himself declared that as soon as his book was published 'I wrote "author" instead of "journalist" in a new passport.'[10]

The day after the wedding the newly married couple flew to New York *en route* for London, with the manuscript of Ian Fleming's first novel included in the luggage.

On 17 June 1952 a report in *The Times* stated that Dennis George Muldowney, a porter at the Reform Club in Pall Mall, had been charged with the murder of Christine Granville, aged thirty-seven, at Lexham Gardens, Kensington, on Sunday, 15 June. Chief Inspector Jennings told the West London Police Court that he had seen the dead body of Christine at the foot of the stairs in the hall of the Shellbourne Hotel, Lexham Gardens. Muldowney made a statement saying: 'I killed her. Let's get away from here and get it over quickly.'

Granville and Muldowney had first met when they were both employed as stewards aboard ship. It would seem that Christine Granville had taken pity on Muldowney because he was a somewhat unhappy character and that, as a result, he had fallen obsessively in love with her. In the subsequent court case Muldowney said that in April of that year he had seen Christine with some other man. 'This upset me very much and I decided I would kill her,' he added. He did not name the man, but added: 'I did not see her again until June 15. . . . She told me she did not want anything to do with me and was off to the Continent and would see me in two years' time. Then I took the knife from the sheath which I had in my hip pocket and stabbed her in the chest.'[11]

On 10 September 1952 Muldowney was sentenced to death at the Old Bailey. He was executed on 30 September. There was no indication from Fleming as to his feelings about this tragedy and he never made any reference to Christine afterwards, as far as I can ascertain. At that time he would not have wished to be linked to this bizarre murder through his relationship with Christine becoming known.

Meanwhile on 12 August that year his son was born. It would appear that Anne left the choice of names to her husband, and the boy was christened Caspar Robert at Chelsea Old Church. Caspar may have been chosen because it was the first name of Admiral of the Fleet Sir Caspar John, son of Fleming's very old acquaintance, Augustus John, the painter. Robert had been the name of Fleming's grandfather as well as that of one of his brothers. But Caspar was a favourite name of Fleming's and he told friends he had chosen it because of Robert Southey's 'apt poetic reference to the timing of my son's birth'. In his poem 'The Battle of Blenheim' Southey wrote: 'It was a summer evening,/Old Kaspar's work was done . . .'

By the end of 1952 all plans had been made for the publication of *Casino Royale* by Jonathan Cape, with a special recommendation from William Plomer, as well as enthusiastic backing from Daniel George, another of Cape's readers. Meanwhile Fleming had taken the advice given to him by Michael Arlen, the popular novelist of the 1920s: 'Write your second book before you see the reviews of your first.'

It was many years afterwards that the events of 1952 began to make rather astonishing sense to me. When in the late 1960s I was doing research into the whole history of the British Secret Service down the ages I spent some time delving into the wartime adventures and exploits of Christine Granville. Billy (W. Stanley) Moss, another British agent who knew her and worked with her, said: 'The almost mesmeric attraction she had for men was a blend of vivacity, flirtatiousness, charm and sheer personality. She could switch that personality on and off like a searchlight that could blind anyone in its beam.'

What puzzled me, however, was that very few people were prepared to talk about her. Some of them avoided the subject, others hinted vaguely and somewhat seriously that this was not a matter which could be discussed. 'It is safer to leave that name alone,' said one. 'No good will come from talking about her.' But no reasons for this attitude were given. As Christine had been regarded as a war hero, it seemed rather silly, especially as her deeds had been written about already. Yet others came up against the same problem – the curtain of silence that descended whenever Christine Granville's name was mentioned. Even those who knew her during the period she was living at the Shellbourne Hotel wouldn't say much about her.

A number of her friends were approached by at least three would-be biographers after her death, but, says Madeleine Masson, in her biography of Christine, 'some of her friends made a pact against biographers'.[12] Certainly other would-be biographers were discouraged by lack of assistance and gave up the self-imposed tasks. Daniel Farson, another author who become fascinated with her story, stated that

> . . . after her death three of her closest wartime colleagues agreed to protect her memory from any glamorization. Largely due to their lack of co-operation, a Hollywood film was abandoned; a biography by a distinguished authoress was shelved; and a TV series seems in abeyance. When I began researching for a radio programme, I was startled by a virulent letter from a well-known writer along the lines that 'there are things that cannot and must not be told'. What could this mean? That Christine Granville was a double agent? The facts deny any such suspicion. Though I am still puzzled, I assume this was a further example of the protection of her memory that amounts to possessiveness.'[13]

There are one or two other mysteries associated with the Granville story. One of her close friends and a mourner at her funeral at the Roman Catholic cemetery at Kensal Green, London, was Countess Teresa Lubienska. She was stabbed to death on the underground station platform at Gloucester Road on 24 May 1957. The reason for her death is still a mystery.

This could be said to be a *non sequitur*. But the various stories surrounding the death of General Sikorski, Commander-in-Chief of the Free Polish Forces, at Gibraltar in July 1943, do positively lead to Granville's name once again. As is well known, the general was killed when the aircraft in which he was travelling failed to take off from the Gibraltar airstrip and crashed into the sea. For many years two stories circulated regarding this event: one was that the murder had been engineered by the British Secret Service because Sikorski was a formidable obstacle to the Allies' relationships with Stalin (a rumour not unnaturally first put about by Joseph Goebbels's German propaganda department); the other was that the Soviet NKVD had instigated the crime. The British official view was that it was an unfortunate accident, largely due to the relatively short runway at Gibraltar airport.

In 1983 a publication titled *Special Office Brief: An Early Warning Intelligence System* stated:

> General Sikorski, the gallant Polish leader, was thrice warned by a loyal senior British general not to fly from Gibraltar to London in the Liberator aircraft in which he was murdered. The general was subsequently openly insulted in London by a Cabinet minister for having warned Sikorski. The brave spy, Christine Granville, who unluckily knew of Sikorski's murder, was given £100 and was forced to find work as a stewardess and ended up stabbed to death.[14]

Why link Granville's name with that of Sikorski, it may be asked, except that they were both Poles? The implication is that Christine Granville not only knew about Sikorski's death but something of the background to it and events connected with it, leading to the conclusion that he was murdered. The report also stated that 'the man who ordered' the murder 'cannot be named. But one day he will be'.

Those who have probed into the story of Sikorski's death have come up against more or less the same hostility and silence as the would-be biographers of Granville. Louis Fitzgibbon, referring to the 'mysterious plane crash', and pointing out that the Soviet Ambassador to Britain, Maisky, was in Gibraltar at the time, stated: 'I spoke to the late Marshal of the R.A.F. Sir John Slessor, who had carried out the investigation [of the Gibraltar plane crash] at the time, and in less than a flash, he said, "Fitzgibbon, drop it." I found that interesting.'[15]

Certainly my own inquiries suggest that Christine Granville had known something of the inside story of the Sikorski affair and, as she told her friend, Olga Bialoguski, she felt certain that she had been victimized because of this. Olga Bialoguski told me: 'Christine once said that Sikorski's death kept on being brought up as some kind of a black mark against her. She said that she had been told that on no account must she talk about it. Who told her this and why this was she did not explain. As the Sikorski affair had happened a long time ago I couldn't see the point in all this and did not press her for information. Perhaps I should have done.'

It is true that General Sir Noel Mason-MacFarlane, Governor of Gibraltar at the time of Sikorski's death, had warned the Polish C-in-C against flying in the aircraft in which he was subsequently killed, though he declined to give any specific reason for doing so. This story was confirmed by Mrs Olga Lisiewicz, who acted as interpreter during MacFarlane's conversation with Sikorski's widow after her husband's death, and she claimed that Mac-Farlane was in 'an exceptionally distressed state' about his failure to impress the seriousness of his warning on the general's pro-posed trip.

When the playwright Rolf Hochhuth wrote a play, *The Soldiers*, implying that Winston Churchill connived at a plot to murder Sikorski, he also suggested that the Czech pilot of the plane, Captain Prchal, was part of the conspiracy. Libel proceedings were then brought against Hochhuth by Prchal, who was awarded £50,000 damages and granted a permanent injunction against Hochhuth. Prchal died in America in 1989. He had promised to leave his papers to Stanford University, but then changed his mind without giving any reason. However, General MacFarlane did eventually leave his papers to the Imperial War Museum and his diaries and other comments on the death of Sikorski give some sidelights on the affair.

One particularly significant item in the diaries was this: 'I knew the pilot – a Czech named Perzl [*sic*] quite well. I had flown with him. . . . One strange fact – this pilot never under any circumstances wore his Mae West, yet when picked out of the water [i.e. following the crash after take-off from Gibraltar] it was on and tied up.'[16]

These may be regarded as divergences from the story of Ian Fleming, but he would have delighted in such a mystery, especially if it was linked to a beautiful spy like Christine Granville. A close examination of *Casino Royale* shows that some of the subjects discussed in the present chapter were woven into it in a most remarkable and unexpected manner. I had always regarded *Casino Royale* as the best and most immaculately written of all Fleming's books, an opinion shared by such good judges as Dennis Wheatley and Roald Dahl. A few years ago I was short of something to read one evening and I decided to look at it again. It was a casual decision: I had no particular reason for reading the book again, but as I did so I began to feel I was reading a true-life story. This first dawned on me when I read about the drink Bond called 'Vesper' after the female spy he had been working with. Says Bond: 'Three measures of Gordon's, one of vodka, half a measure of Kina Lillet. Shake it very well until it's ice-cold, then add a large thin slice of lemon-peel. Got it?'

But there was much more to come. As I kept turning the pages surprise after surprise confronted me. Some I appreciated straight away, others called for further research, which I lost no time in carrying out. For example there was the name of Vesper Lynd. As already noted in the epigraph, Fleming writes in *Casino Royale* that Vesper Lynd excused her name by saying: 'It's rather a bore always having to explain, but I was born in the evening, on a very stormy evening, according to my parents. Apparently they wanted to remember it.' Further inquiries established the fact that Christine Granville was born on a stormy night and that her father had given her the nickname of 'Vespérale', or, as he himself explained, 'qui a rapport au soir clarté vespérale'.[17]

Fleming describes Vesper as speaking French 'like a native'.
According to others who knew her, Christine spoke French
flawlessly. He also refers to her hair as being 'very black and . . .
low on the nape of the neck' and mentions her 'deep blue' eyes
and 'wide and sensual' mouth. These are fair descriptions of
Christine. As I turned the pages I soon became convinced that
Vesper was indeed based on this remarkable heroine of the
Second World War. Vesper says in her last letter to James Bond:

> I was in love with a Pole in the R.A.F. Until you, I still was.
> You can find out who he was. He had two D.S.O.s. and after
> the war he was trained by M and dropped back into Poland.
> They caught him and by torturing him they found out a lot and
> also about me. They came after me and told me he could live if
> I would work for them. He knew nothing of this, but he was
> allowed to write to me. The letter arrived on the fifteenth of
> each month. I found I couldn't stop. I couldn't bear the idea of
> a fifteenth coming round without his letter. It would mean that I
> had killed him. I tried to give them as little as possible. . . .

Fiction, of course, but then for years Christine too had a very
great friend and colleague who was Polish, the gallant Andrezej
Kowerski, who served in the British Army, not the RAF. Vesper
served in the WRNS while Granville was officially in the WAAF
as a cover for her work in Special Operations Executive. It is
peculiarly noticeable how Bond changes from distinct irritation at
having to work with Vesper to something like passionate involve-
ment with her as the narrative progresses. Perhaps this reflected
Fleming's forebodings about his coming marriage which occupied
his mind as he started the book. He was trying to escape from such
thoughts and Vesper was the theme that beckoned him away from
them.

By page 180 of *Casino Royale* (Cape edition) there is a different
tone altogether. No longer is it a case of women getting in the way
and fogging things up, as Bond puts it, but

> He found he could speak to her easily and he was surprised.
>     With most women his manner was a mixture of taciturnity
> and passion. The lengthy approaches to a seduction bored him

almost as much as the subsequent mess of disentanglement. He found something grisly in the inevitability of the pattern of each affair. . . .

But with Vesper there could be none of this
. . . her presence was each day an oasis of pleasure,
something to look forward to. In their talk there was nothing
but companionship with a distinct undertone of passion.


By this time there is only one discordant note. Bond, like Fleming, does not like flowers in any of his rooms either at work or at home. Vesper sends him flowers. The build-up of a passionate and sincere love affair for Vesper continues right up to the end of Fleming's story. By Chapter XXVI Bond is actually talking to Vesper of marriage. But by the next chapter Vesper is dead, having left behind a letter to 'My darling James' in which she admits that she was a double agent working for the Russians as well as the British. The last paragraph of the book has Bond speaking on the telephone: 'Pass this on at once. 3030 was a double, working for Redland. . . . The bitch is dead now.'

All of which poses many intriguing questions. Fleming put all of himself into the character of Bond in that first book, much more so than in subsequent novels. 'James Bond suddenly knew that he was tired. He always knew when his body or his mind had had enough.' By that time Fleming had already had the first tingling warnings of heart trouble. He refers to Bond lighting up 'his seventieth cigarette of the day' and on another occasion to Bond's 'first cigarette, a Balkan and Turkish mixture made for him by Morlands of Grosvenor Street'. That was where Fleming got his cigarettes and he was a heavy smoker. But how much is Vesper's character based on that of Christine Granville? Did Fleming write this novel to try to eliminate her from his system, to put an end to a love affair? Or did he conjure it all up as a kind of joke which, he hoped, when he sent a copy of his book to Christine, she could smilingly share with him? Alas, that was something which was not to be.

'Good heavens, Vesper', says Bond, 'you look absolutely splendid. You must thrive on disaster.' Christine, according to all her friends and colleagues, thrived on disaster too.

Did Granville try to play a Vesper trick on Fleming in some mysterious way and was this his attempt to get even with her? The last sentence of the book seems deliberately nasty: 'The bitch is dead now.' But one must remember that this was written before Christine was murdered. There is little point in pursuing conspiracy theories, or pondering whether Christine's death at the hands of a schizophrenic porter was in some way manipulated by someone in the underworld of espionage. Yet as a footnote to this whole intriguing game of finding answers to a non-stop puzzle there is the evidence of Mr 'Teddy' Knight (formerly of the Polish Air Force Association), who saw Christine in a West End club the night before she was murdered. 'She was talking to a well-dressed Russian woman,' he told me.

# 10

## *Peace-time Adventurer*

I have adventures more or less mapped out – a real treasure
hunt in the Seychelles, the Great Cave of Niah in North
Borneo, gold smuggling in Macao and so forth.[1]

The memorandum just quoted was typical of Fleming's life
from 1952 onwards – books the top priority, adventure a
close second. It had been suggested he should do a series of
articles entitled 'Round the World in Eight Adventures'. He was
determined to succeed as a profitable writer, though he was somewhat impatient with the relatively modest sales of the first edition
of *Casino Royale*. 'My profits from *Casino Royale*', he wrote on 15
May 1953, 'will just about keep Anne in asparagus over Corona-
tion week.'[2]

Treasure-hunting continued to fascinate him. He seized on the
name of Cockatoo Island, Buccaneer Archipelago, Yampi Sound,
in the India Ocean. It sounded wildly romantic, he commented.
Could it be an island where treasure was supposed to be buried?
Alas, I had to reply after making some inquiries, it belonged to
Australia and it was full not of buried treasure but of iron and
steel which the Australians were turning out at the rate of 25 million
tons a year. His inquiry was typical of his restless and eternal quest
for commitment of one kind or another. His urge to make a success
of his books was in part a reaction to the realization that, however
good his Mercury foreign service might be, Kemsley Newspapers
were on the decline and sooner or later a take-over was probable.
Like most of us who had had careers interrupted by wartime
service, he realized that the battle to win in peace-time was far
harder than the war in which we had all fought.

Fleming told Ken W. Purdy, the American: 'I sleep tranquilly, but I'm certainly neurotic in many respects. I think that to be a creative writer, or a creative anything else, you've got to be neurotic in some degree. I'm not quite certain where I'm neurotic, but I am.'

Perhaps there was a degree of hyperbole in this statement and Fleming might have been nearer the truth if he had substituted 'restless' for 'neurotic'. But this was his way of gently debunking himself, which he quite enjoyed doing. Without question he was a sensitive person, though he would have winced at the description. He was a man who essentially needed to feel free as well as to be free.

While many, if not most authors, think it is quite enough to write a book and that taking part in its promotion is an awful bore, Fleming, whatever he may have thought, took a keen and forthright interest in the production, promotion and the rights problems of all his work. This may have been partly a result of his realization of the insecurity of authorship. Norman Lewis, the travel writer and a friend of Fleming, stated in his book, *A View of the World*, that 'Jonathan Cape himself much disliked Ian Fleming's writing and refused to meet him, and could only be persuaded to publish his books by a united front established in Fleming's favour by the firm's other directors, and by William Plomer, their reader.'

This made Fleming only more determined to succeed. From early on it was evident that he was looking ahead to the day when he would be able to count his sales in millions. This was not a matter of greed but of his memory of early days on low pay and how it affected him. In the same way towards the end of his life he left the way open for another writer to carry on his books in the event of his death. No doubt he was thinking of the future of his son Caspar just as much as his wife. It was not that he was arrogant about the prospect of a successful career as a novelist and writer, but that he felt it was up to him to ensure there were no slip-ups either in the promotion of his work or the routine and style in which each book was produced. He was quick to admit when he made mistakes in his writing, as is shown in a letter he sent to Michael Howard of Jonathan Cape: 'It is really ghastly. I have never made so many mistakes as in OHMSS. Here is a total list of all the corrections which should go into the next edition.'[3]

Equally he took a keen and personal interest in the designs for dust-jackets of his books. On one occasion he made the comment that 'the colours should be as bold as he can possibly make them and I'm prepared to sacrifice the grey-blue of J.B.'s eyes for a brighter blue, if Dickie would prefer it'. Referring to the dust-jacket of *For Your Eyes Only*, he said that these words 'should be stamped on a portion of a document – at the top of it and not interfering with the text – and I enclose a draft of how this might look on a real document and with words which would be appropriate to the story. The title should be red and perhaps rather fuzzy as if it really was a rubber stamp'.[4]

He had a habit, whether in journalism or in dealing with publishers and people anxious for foreign rights, to turn his firmness and toughness into a joke. Sometimes this was misunderstood, though once one knew his foibles it was easy to detect the meaning. 'Please explain to these people that nowadays I light my cigarettes with £100 notes,' he wrote to Michael Howard. This was not meant to be an arrogant comment but merely a warning that he could not be fobbed off with any transparently low offers.

Fleming's married life, superficially at least, seemed to be on an even keel for the first two years. His lease of White Cliffs, St Margaret's Bay, which Fleming had taken over from Noël Coward in 1951, provided a weekend retreat. Yet though Fleming loved the place, his wife did not. She thought it much too small for the large-scale entertaining in which she loved to indulge. Anne Fleming had described the place to Evelyn Waugh as 'seaweed in the sitting room'. In London the Flemings had taken over a house in Victoria Square, close to Victoria Station. This was a relatively small abode and had a number of storeys with steep flights of stairs and no lift. Fleming's study was at the top of the house and it was to this room that he immediately escaped when on returning from the office he found those downstairs crowded with Anne's party guests.

These frequent parties soon became an impediment to a happy marriage. It had been by playing the hostess in a big way throughout her life that Anne had gathered around her such a wide circle of friends, ranging from Sir John Sparrow, Warden of All Souls, and Isaiah Berlin on the one side to Evelyn Waugh and Francis Bacon, as well as innumerable politicians and their wives, on the other. Fleming's escape-hole from these parties consisted of a bedroom and study combined. There he would remain until all had gone. Thursday was usually the day upon which the major party of the week would be held, and it was to this that various literary and socialite people were invited. Fleming complained that his wife was 'too often surrounded by queers' and he was particularly furious when a certain guest told her that he had a date with what Ian called 'a rent boy' and Anne told him to bring the boy back to the party.

Nevertheless they shared some happy breaks together, and they both seemed to enjoy life best when travelling overseas. In the spring of 1954 Ian took Anne by car through Provence to Marseilles, where he intended to interview Commandant Jacques Yves Cousteau. At that time Cousteau was exploring the wreck of a Greek trading vessel off the coast and Fleming's intention was to deep dive personally to the wreck. He had become particularly interested in deep-sea diving from the late 1940s when I reported to him some of the plans of Professor Piccard's deep-sea diving bathyscaphe which was then lying off Dakar in French West Africa. While at that time he welcomed news stories on this subject, I felt that his interest also extended to the field of Intelligence, for Piccard's diving experiments were arousing some considerable controversy. Piccard's plan to attempt the ocean diving record in his self-propelled 15-ton metal observation diving bell was abandoned at first because of faulty equipment. The original plan had been sponsored by the Belgian Government. Later it was reported that a new attempt would be made in the Mediterranean under joint French and Belgian naval sponsorhip. Then came news of a problem: Professor Max Cosyns, Piccard's chief assistant, who was director of the Belgian centre of nuclear research, had attended the communist-sponsored World Peace Conference in Paris. It was strongly urged that Cosyns should be asked to withdraw from the new experiment.

From then on Fleming followed such schemes with the keenest interest, particularly as it became clear that French Intelligence was leading the way in realizing the importance of the underwater detection of nuclear-armed submarines. Some of the French experts in this field felt that from a purely economic viewpoint underseas exploration was important, while French Intelligence had been the first to detect Soviet interest in the subject. Later French Intelligence benefited greatly from the underwater researches of Cousteau, the marine archaeologist and former captain in the French Navy who established the Underseas Research Group as early as 1945 and in 1950 became president of the *Campagnes Océanographiques Françaises*.

Fleming was fascinated by Cousteau and had a great admiration for him. After France's surrender Cousteau had stayed in the Navy in occupied France, but had also worked for the Underground Services. Once, posing as an Italian officer, he had led a party into the Italian headquarters at Sète and spent four tense hours photographing a code-book and top-secret papers. Yet he disliked espionage work and maintained that ever since the war his aim had been to obtain information from the depths of the ocean, not to interpret it. In his ship *Calypso* he made annual oceanographic expeditions and took part in the making of the bathyscaphe, first with Piccard and then with the French Navy. On the occasion of his visit to Marseilles, Fleming sailed off with Cousteau but found that diving to such depths gave him headaches. His wife stayed with Somerset Maugham while waiting for his return.

Doubtless Fleming still kept Naval Intelligence informed with any worthwhile information he picked up either through journalistic contacts or his own ever keen fact-finding trips. He had positive ideas as to how naval intelligence should be conducted in the post-war years and these he would sometimes express at meetings of the Thirty-Six Club, which comprised former members of Admiral Godfrey's staff. At one such club meeting (usually conducted at a cocktail session, with dinner to follow) the late Vice-Admiral Sir Norman Denning recalled Fleming saying that 'the whole organisation of Intelligence wanted revolutionising and he still saw a use for the traditional spy of fiction'.[5]

Donald McLachlan, referring to another meeting of the Thirty-Six Club, seemed to bear this out when he commented that 'Ian held forth thus: If he was D.N.I., he said, he would run Intelligence in such and such a way. This "such" world was the world of his novels'.[6]

Fleming's name has even been linked to the mysterious case of Commander Crabb and his diving exploits underneath the Soviet cruiser *Ordzhonikidze* in Portsmouth harbour in April 1956, though as far as one can tell in only a joking manner. Commander Crabb, one of the Royal Navy's best underwater sabotage experts and divers, dived into Portsmouth harbour on a secret mission near the cruiser which had brought Khrushchev and Bulganin, the Soviet leaders, to Britain. Crabb never reported back to duty and his disappearance caused a parliamentary storm. There were, of course, the usual denials that Crabb was operating on behalf of British Intelligence, with some rather snide hints that he might have been a free-lance agent for the Americans. Later, despite the fact that a body was reported to have been washed ashore near Chichester and was, on the flimsiest of evidence, confirmed as his, there were reports that he had been seen living in the USSR under a Russian name.

In private, Randolph Churchill, Winston's son, jocularly proclaimed that Ian Fleming had something to do with the Portsmouth 'prank', even referring to 'Frogman Fleming' and his exploits in connection with the Crabb affair in an amusing skit in an American magazine. True, the article was fictitious satire, but Randolph had an unerring nose for embarrassing gossip of this kind. The only light I can throw on this suggestion is that at the time of the Portsmouth incident Fleming was supposed to be taking a cure at a health farm, yet in fact he was not then at the address he named when telephoned there. Whether he had another alibi, I cannot say. Certainly the Crabb episode would have been the kind of intelligence-gathering stunt that might well have appealed to him as a keen underwater explorer, though he was not in too good a state of health at the time.

Yet I think Fleming was quite well informed on this whole affair and, while ever keen to make the most of scoops, he put what he would regard as the national interest first. This was especially the case with reference to Anglo-American relations in the field of Intelligence which had been so severely upset by the Burgess and Maclean defection. His colleague Ernest Cuneo, Vice-President of the news agency, NANA, was a serious-minded man who had maintained his own links with US Intelligence circles. My information at the time was that the Russians had been tipped off about Crabb's secret mission before it took place and that they had taken him prisoner. On that basis I wrote a story for NANA suggesting that Crabb was still alive and might turn up in Moscow. Fleming deleted my story altogether (as European Vice-President of NANA he kept close control over all material from Mercury which was syndicated to the agency). He insisted that Crabb was undoubtedly dead, either killed by the Soviets or drowned. My story might well have been misinterpreted in the United States; in other words, the Americans could have taken the view that Crabb was a defector not a victim.

Government papers on the Crabb affair have been locked away with a hundred years' ban on their publication, which seems ridiculous considering that the Cold War is now over. Fleming, I recall, shook his head in doubt some fourteen months later over the inquest verdict that the body found off Chichester was Crabb's, while later he also dismissed various attempts to smear Crabb with allegations that he had defected to the USSR as 'total nonsense'. 'I hope someone will try to clear Crabb's name one day,' he told me. This view is identical with that of Rear-Admiral Nicholas Poland, who has written a history of Royal Navy underwater warfare. The Admiral considers it grossly unfair that the Government will not allow the name of a gallant officer to be cleared. In 1962 Rear-Admiral Poland was Director of Underwater Sea Warfare at the Ministry of Defence.

Equally, of course, Fleming tried in his Bond stories – especially the early ones – to stress in the public mind a cordial relationship between the British SIS and the American CIA. One has only to remember Felix Leiter in *Casino Royale*.

Large parties Fleming may not have liked, but he mixed in a variety of circles and was as much at ease among intellectuals as with men of action, taking care in both cases to ask them searching questions to find out what made them tick. Roald Dahl spoke of his talent for 'turning a casual conversation into a sparkling occasion'. During one of their meetings Fleming suggested in one such conversation the basis of a plot which Dahl later used in his *Tales of the Unexpected*. The story was typical of that black humour which Ian had inherited during his naval days. It described how a man murdered his wife by bludgeoning her with a frozen joint of meat and later served up the same joint, duly cooked, to the unsuspecting police investigator.

Though these were the years of the author, Fleming tried to make them the years of the adventurer too. His aim was always to get fun and adventure out of his researches for his books. There was his trip to the Pyrenees in 1953 when, at the age of forty-five, he joined an expedition to descend into the second deepest cave in the world. He must have been exceedingly frustrated when he was allowed to stand only at the entrance and watch, especially after a four hours' climb. In October 1954 he visited Alcatraz, Nevada, Las Vegas and Los Angeles to collect material for *Diamonds Are Forever*. *Moonraker* was also plotted out in Las Vegas amidst the world of the twenty-four-hour divorce and gambling. 'A happy escape from Victoria Square which is frequently being festooned with effeminate intellectuals,' he once said, referring to these jaunts abroad. Yet it was not only at his wife Anne's parties that he found such company tiresome. When he was in Tangier in 1957, working on his series of articles, *The Diamond Smugglers*, which was serialized in *The Sunday Times*, he wrote home, saying: 'My life has revolved around a place called Dean's Bar . . . there's nothing but pansies and I have been fresh meat for them. I'm fed up with buggers. They do absolutely nothing all day long but complain about each other and arrange flowers.'[7]

Fleming had made the acquaintance of Sir Percy Sillitoe, the former head of MI5, who was winding up IDSO (International Diamond Security Organization), a private company he had set up after retiring from MI5. Fleming inscribed the flyleaf of his personal copy of *The Diamond Smugglers* thus: 'This was written in two weeks in Tangiers, April, 1957. Sir Percy Sillitoe sold the story to the *Sunday Times* and I had to write it. . . . It was a good story until all the possible libel was cut out. There was nearly an injunction against me and the *Sunday Times* by De Beers to prevent publication. . . . It is adequate journalism but a poor book and necessarily rather contrived, though the facts are true.'[8]

This was not the only occasion when Fleming came up against legal problems in the course of his writing. His one unpublished book is proof of this. It exists only in typescript of some 145 large quarto pages and it is entitled 'State of Excitement: Impressions of Kuwait'. He completed it in December 1960, and in an explanatory note he says:

> It was a condition of my obtaining facilities to visit Kuwait and write the book that the text should have the approval of the Kuwait Oil Company, whose guest I was. The Oil Company expressed approval of the book but felt it their duty to submit the typescript to members of the Kuwait Government for their approval. The Sheikhs concerned found unpalatable certain mild comments and criticisms and particularly the passages referring to the adventurous past of the country which now wishes to be 'civilised' in every respect and forget the romantic origins. Accordingly the book was stillborn. The copyright is the property of the Kuwait Oil Company and may not be set up in print or quoted from without the written approval of the Company.[9]

On his visits to the United States Fleming submitted his own ideas of how to gather intelligence. 'He was always brimming with ingenious schemes for improving the whole system of Intelligence,' Ernest Cuneo told me. 'He was eager that the CIA should actually advertise for defectors in various newspapers around the world. "Do that and you will pave the way for a break-up of the whole Soviet system," he said. I believe he put up the same plan to the FBI and told them where to advertise.'

In 1989 the New York office of the FBI started advertising in the local Russian language paper for KGB agents or anyone who knew anything about Soviet Intelligence work to come and offer their services. 'Six people have already telephoned the number provided in *Novoye Russkoye Slove* which is aimed at the tens of thousands of recent Soviet immigrants who now live in the New

York area, the F.B.I. said yesterday,' reported the New York correspondent of *The Times*.[10] Eventually Fleming's suggestion proved practical in American eyes.

Adventures in these years ranged from natural history excursions to interviewing gangsters. Ivar Bryce and Fleming were often thinking up such projects, sometimes to be carried out jointly. There was the trip they made in 1956 to a remote island in the Bahamas to count flamingos. In May 1960 Fleming went to Naples in quest of background material on the Mafia and drug-peddling. He even managed to get an interview with 'Lucky' Luciano, the former American gangster who had been sent back to Italy by the Americans. They sipped China tea together. Luciano told Fleming that he had been framed and unfairly sentenced for white slavery.

The gradual demise of various Kemsley newspapers during this period was undoubtedly unsettling for Fleming. The main excuse for the world-wide Mercury service was the fact that Lord Kemsley owned so many papers. But the disappearance of the *Daily Sketch*, the *Sunday Graphic*, the *Sunday Chronicle* and, finally, the *Empire News*, changed everything. Mercury from then onwards was concentrated entirely on *The Sunday Times*; it was not considered worth while servicing the provincial papers with Mercury's foreign news and features. Fleming himself turned his attention to running the 'Atticus' gossip column of *The Sunday Times*, which had at various times been written by John Buchan, Sacheverell Sitwell and Sir Robert Bruce Lockhart. The column had become staid and lacking in any sparkle, but Fleming soon changed all that, even managing to obtain from Lord Kemsley freedom to fashion the column in his own way and to mention in it anyone he liked. This was a major concession in those days.

He had for a long time taken a keen interest in the quarterly magazine *The Book Collector*, and he was also a director of the Queen Anne Press, owned by Lord Kemsley, which published it. In 1955 Kemsley decided that publishing *The Book Collector* was no longer economically justifiable. Fleming immediately offered to buy it and the deal was clinched for a mere £50. He did not play an active role with *The Book Collector*, leaving the editorship to his friend John Hayward.

Fleming's suggestions and advice on book collecting have already been noted, but in these latter years he had developed new ideas for would-be collectors. He once told me that just collecting books alone can be rather dull. The aim should be to make it exciting. Study a book you like, ask yourself if there is a story behind the book. Try to find out that story either by making your own inquiries and checking back with the author, or sometimes the other way around. Add the documented details of your discoveries of the story behind the story and you will increase the value of your book. Evelyn Waugh's books provided a good example of what he was talking about. 'Take Captain Grimes in *Decline and Fall*. He is a real person and his name is William Young. One day his story will be really interesting.'

I eventually discovered that William Young, who died in 1971, was indeed the model for Captain Grimes. Instead of drowning in a bog while escaping from prison, however, he died in a Church of England home for the destitute. It came as a shock to the home when they learned that in his will he left £58,557.

Another literary character who fascinated Fleming was Sadie Thompson, the prostitute featured in Somerset Maugham's novel *Rain* (1921; published in 1928 as *Sadie Thompson*). He had discovered that Maugham had used the actual name of an itinerant whore who lived in Bella Bartley's boarding-house in Pago Pago in 1916–17. Maugham, so Fleming told me, had occupied an adjacent room to Sadie's in this boarding-house in the Iwi Lei red-light district of Honolulu. The late Benjamin Franklin Kneubuhl, an American merchant in Pago Pago, had confirmed this to Fleming, saying: 'She arrived here from Honolulu in the early part of December 1916. Maugham came on the same boat with her, together with a couple of London Missionary Society pastors and their wives, just like it is told in the story.' Maugham's biographer, Ted Morgan, subsequently confirmed that Maugham arrived in Pago Pago in the same ship as Sadie Thompson on 5 December 1916.[11]

Fleming delved much more deeply into this story, urging me to make inquiries in Samoa. The real story of Sadie Thompson turned out to be that she fell in love with the orderly of the Fita-fita guard who was running errands for the governor. When their liaison was discovered, the orderly was confined to barracks. Sadie smuggled a message through to him. This read: 'Joe, honey, I'm really leaving in the *Ventura*. When you're ready to come to Honolulu, I'll pay your fare'; and she gave him an address in Kalalaua Avenue in Waikiki, Honolulu. But by the time Joe arrived in Honolulu many years later, Sadie had long since de-parted. As for Joe, he ended up with the rank of High Chief living in Tutuila Island.

The point which Fleming was anxious to make was that such research into the real identity of fictional characters can be a fascinating hobby and at the same time such material, duly documented, can greatly enhance the value of a first edition. It is a hobby that can be practised indefinitely and is rewarding in every sense of the word.

When he was undertaking his *Thrilling Cities* series of articles Fleming paid his first visit to Hong Kong, where his guide and mentor was his chief Far East correspondent Richard Hughes, who had covered the Korean War for Mercury. Though totally different in almost every respect, they got along admirably and Hughes not only showed him around Hong Kong but took him by ferry to the Portuguese colony of Macao. Fleming told Hughes that he regarded the whole trip as something he would 'cherish for evermore'. When Hughes took him to the Luk Kwok area of Hong Kong, to take a look at what Hughes typically and amus-ingly termed 'the family girls', business was dull and some of the girls were knitting. 'Ian took a reporter's interest in the signs: "Girls, But No Obligation to Buy Drinks! Clean Surroundings! Take It Easy! You Are at Home! Fine Food and Wines! Enjoy to the Maximum at the Least Expenses!"' wrote Hughes. 'But he seemed to be more taken with the Siamese fighting-fish in the huge bowl than with the Suzie Wongs in their small cubicles.'[12]

The visit to Macao was to find out something about the racket in gold. A fortune in gold was passing through the Shin Hang Bank year after year: the bullion came openly and legally from all parts of the world to Hong Kong, whence it was transported to Macao, again legally and openly. Portugal did not belong to the Inter-national Monetary Fund and was not subject to the Fund's regula-tions on the import of gold. But what happened afterwards was illegal. The bullion was melted down and turned into 9-ounce gold bars which were easily smuggled through or around Hong Kong to illicit buyers all around the world. Fleming was fascinated by this story and even interviewed the late Dr Pedro Jose Lobo, who was directly concerned with the gold racket. He included his conversation with Dr Lobo in his *Thrilling Cities* series.

In 1959 Fleming went to Japan in quest of background material for *You Only Live Twice*, in which he based his Australian secret agent character, Dikko Henderson, on Hughes. At the Imperial Hotel in Tokyo he met Somerset Maugham and they spent a whole day together, visiting the Kodokan gymnasium, a ju-jitsu establishment where fifty young men were practising break-falls, while in another room a group of girls obligingly staged a mock fight. 'On the next floor, in one vast hall,' writes Ted Morgan, recording this visit, they were entertained by 'two hundred bouts . . . . In another room a class for children between eight and ten was being conducted by a red belt, who showed a boy of ten how he was to use his leverage to bring down someone twice his size, while half a dozen doting mothers sat on benches and watched.'[13]

Anne Fleming's comment on this trip to Japan was that 'poor Thunderbird', as she called Ian, 'couldn't get a girl in Japan because he doesn't know the language'. However, Fleming must inevitably have met some Japanese women who spoke English, and in fact he once made James Bond say that, if ever he married, it would be to an 'air hostess', as they were always 'tucking you up' and 'bringing you hot meals' and 'they're always smiling and wanting to please'. This is actually a fair enough description of Japanese air hostesses, who all speak excellent English. Note, too, that Bond said his second choice for a wife would be a Japanese woman: 'They seem to have the right idea, too.'

Maugham, cynical though he could often be about other people's books, had written to Fleming after reading *Casino Royale*, saying:

I started it last night in bed and at half past one, when I was about half way through, I said to myself: I really must get some sleep, though what I really wanted to do was to read on to the end. I finished it an hour ago. It goes with a swing from the first

page to the last and is really thrilling. . . . You really managed
to get the tension to the highest possible pitch.'[14]


All these adventures in the late 1950s were in part at least an
excuse to escape from the interminable parties given by his wife,
and from marriage too. There was also disagreement between them
concerning the way their son Caspar was being brought up. Fleming
felt that he was hopelessly spoilt by his mother. Caspar did not see
very much of his father; rather more in the holidays in Jamaica than
anywhere else. At home in England the Flemings spent Monday to
Friday at the Victoria Square house in London, and only at weekends did they join Caspar, his governess and nanny in Kent.

Miss Mona Potterton, who was with the Flemings in Jamaica
and England and acted as governess to Caspar prior to his being
sent to Summer Fields School, Oxford, remembers them as 'very
good employers who backed up the governess'. She recalls Ian
Fleming returning home from France and organizing a treasure-
hunt in the garden at their home near Canterbury. This treasure-
hunt was designed for Caspar, his nanny and governess, the
objects they had to find being boxes of chocolates from Le
Touquet. As a consequence of Anne Fleming's increasing dislike
of the St Margaret's Bay retreat which her husband loved, in 1958
they left and bought the Old Palace at Bekesbourne. This was a
curious old house which was said to be haunted; a disused tunnel
from it purportedly led to Canterbury Cathedral.

At weekends Anne would usually take Caspar out for picnics
while Ian played golf. In England during the summer Fleming
decided that Caspar ought to have practice at throwing and
catching balls before playing cricket at his preparatory school. 'So
in the afternoons Caspar and I would go into the garden of the
Old Palace with a ball,' said Miss Potterton. 'Neither of us was
at all interested in throwing and catching! Caspar was a very
congenial pupil and relations between us were normally wonder-
fully harmonious, but the catching practice made him rather cross
and I was accused of organising it to annoy him, to which I
somewhat indignantly replied that I was only doing it because I
believed it to be my duty.'[15]

Miss Potterton also recalls that Fleming was very keen for Caspar to enjoy the trip when they went to Jamaica.

> He told me that if I enjoyed myself Caspar would enjoy the holiday more. I can also recall Mr Fleming being rather concerned because he didn't think Caspar was eating properly at Goldeneye, and exclaiming about it in French. Mr Fleming, by the way, would have been happy for the seven-years-old Caspar to have a go at reading his novels, but Mrs Fleming, Nanny and I said no, Mrs Fleming observing that they had an X Certificate![16]

As time went on Ian and Anne to a large extent lived separate lives. He was by this time extremely worried about her disregard for the facts of life concerning their finances. On 20 January 1958 he had written to her from Goldeneye, saying: 'Living on our combined incomes means that we shall not have more than five thousand a year . . . one can live well on that in one house, but not in two.'[17]

It would seem that his wife did pose financial problems for him, as two years later she was complaining to Evelyn Waugh that Ian was on the Sandwich Golf Club committee and 'his only happiness is pink gin, golf clubs and men . . . he wants to keep a flat here and build a rabbit hutch for me instead of a mansion. . . . Shall I force him to build the mansion?'[18]

Eventually Anne got her own way and the Flemings acquired Sevenhampton House, a large, dilapidated Jacobean-style building on the side of a slope, situated some distance from Swindon. It required considerable work to restore it to something worthwhile and much of the house had to be demolished in the process. The surroundings also needed some further work, as there was an unkempt mass of trees, some of them broken, and a lake that needed dredging. Anne set about this task vigorously and told friends that she hoped they would find the money to pay the bills. In the circumstances it is not surprising that Ian took the prudent measure to safeguard funds for the future, including the setting up of Glidrose Productions.

One surprising quirk of Anne's was her sudden dislike of Noël

Coward, whose company she had once greatly enjoyed and who had been what Cole Lesley, Coward's biographer, had described as a 'sympathetic conspirator' in her lengthy romance with Fleming. Coward had composed a most amusing ditty about her marriage and Lesley declared that Coward 'loved them both [Ian and his wife] dearly'.[19] Despite this Anne Fleming wrote to Cecil Beaton about her dislike of Coward, claiming that 'my only false relationships are with him and Rosamond Lehmann and I cannot extricate myself from either'. Judging from what Anne Fleming told other people, and this would seem to be confirmed by Coward's latest biographer, Clive Fisher, she even made the preposterous claim that Coward lusted after her husband. This may, however, have been one of her more curious jokes.

The answer to some of these puzzling comments seems to have been supplied, in part at least, by Loelia, Lady Lindsay of Dowhill, formerly the Duchess of Westminster. Her story is as follows:

Ian was always having little affairs, not serious, but silly little encounters, and he had one with Rosamond Lehmann and he asked Rosamond Lehmann to come and stay in Jamaica. Anne didn't really want her (she only liked close friends) and Ian was too cowardly to tell her for ages that Rosamond Lehmann was coming, and so by the time he did tell her there was no question of putting her off. Well, Rosamond Lehmann had this terrible setback in love with the poet Cecil Day Lewis, who had chucked her for a younger woman, and she was absolutely down the drain and so she was very vulnerable. . . .

Ian saw this wasn't going to go at all, and so he then went off to Noël Coward and said, 'You must ask Rosamond to stay. I simply can't have her. It's too unpleasant.' So Noël said 'I'll think it over', and he came over the next day. 'Yes, I think I'll settle for the polaroid camera you've got.'

Ian said, 'Oh well, I don't know.' So Noël said he couldn't do anything; so Ian said, 'Well, all right, the polaroid camera.' And Noël said, 'And the tripod, too.'

'Not *the* tripod!' 'Yes, the tripod. . . .' And this deal was all fixed up with the wretched woman in front of them and she never, never knew.[20]

Nor were matters helped by Anne's snide remarks about Ian's books and his writing. Far from sympathizing with him when he was being savagely attacked by some critics for sadism and pornography in his work *The Spy Who Loved Me*, she merely commented that he was 'in decline'. This was his most experimental Bond story, in which he diverged from his usual formula. Lady Lindsay commented that Anne 'despised the books. Of course they made all that lovely lolly. But by then she was really bored with him and had that great secret walk-out with Gaitskell'.[21]

Hugh Gaitskell, then leader of the Labour Party, had met Anne Fleming in the first place at one of her parties. This swiftly developed into a close friendship and she became devoted to him, and he to her. 'My ever devoted admirer,' she dubbed him to her closest friends. Often Anne Fleming and Hugh Gaitskell would be downstairs deep in conversation at Victoria Square and Ian would climb wearily to his study without a word. In 1962 Gaitskell suddenly became seriously ill with a mysterious illness. In December of that year he was admitted to Manor House Hospital with what was diagnosed as viral pneumonia. After a week he was discharged and pronounced sufficiently recovered to make an arranged trip to Moscow, having been invited by Khrushchev himself. But he had a relapse the same evening and in January was admitted to the Middlesex Hospital, where he died on the eighteenth of that month. Anne visited him at both hospitals and two days before his death she was so concerned about his state of health that she demanded to see his wife. The inference was that Anne was desperately worried that the true nature of his illness did not seem to have been discovered.

An autopsy revealed that Gaitskell had been suffering from a rare complaint called systemic lupus erythematosus, which affected both the heart and the kidneys, though this was not recorded as such on his death certificate. It then transpired that he had visited the Soviet Embassy in quest of a visa shortly before he became ill: he had been kept waiting for half an hour and was then given coffee and biscuits. 'One of the doctors who treated Gaitskell was so puzzled by the symptoms that he contacted MI5 to report the fact that the disease that killed him was very rare in temperate zones, especially in males and particularly so in those over forty,' states Chapman Pincher. 'As a result a security officer was sent down to the Microbiological Research Establishment – the so-called Germ Warfare Station – and then to the Chemical Defence Establishment at Porton on Salisbury Plain, but experts there could offer no information suggesting that the Russians knew how to induce the disease which is not an infection but caused by the victim's own antibodies.'[22]

Whether Gaitskell died naturally or was murdered as a result of Soviet tactics is a mystery that has never been satisfactorily solved. His widow seemed satisfied that he died a natural death, but, judging from Anne Fleming's own alarm about his case, it seems probable that Gaitskell may have confided his own doubts and suspicions to her when they talked in hospital. He was a moderate socialist who had no sympathy with the USSR and it would have been in the interests of the Soviets to see him removed and another man take his place as leader of the Labour Party.

# 11

## Last Years and the Legacy

Cyril Connolly once said that no writer could be called great until 25 years after his death. By this reckoning Ian Fleming is almost ripe for reassessment. Whether or not his work merits the accolade of literary distinction, there can be no doubt that his books qualify on grounds of longevity. His name . . . is almost as well known today as it was in 1964.[1]

Gaitskell's death came as a blow to Anne Fleming and she remained under stress for some time afterwards. By now Ian Fleming too had been under great stress from a variety of causes over a number of years, not the least being the gradual deterioration in his health. There had been an unfortunate court case in which his mother, now at an advanced age, had been involved. Mrs Evelyn Fleming had become engaged in 1953 to the Marquess of Winchester, who was approaching ninety and financially down on his luck. The following year he quixotically married Miss Bapsy Pavry, sister of the High Priest of the Parsees. At that time Mrs Fleming had set herself up in the Bahamas, and it was to her house there that she invited the Marquess when, a few months after his marriage, he begged 'to be rescued'. In 1954 the new Marchioness of Winchester sued Mrs Fleming for enticing her husband. This quite extraordinary case dragged on until 1958 when finally Mrs Fleming won after it had gone to the Appeal Court. Ian Fleming and his brothers not only gave loyal support to their mother, they sat with her through the hearings.

But it was the Thunderball court case which put the greatest strain on Fleming and it was while this affair was dragging on that he suffered an acute heart attack during a *Sunday Times* conference.

Xanadu Productions had been formed by Ivar Bryce and Kevin McClory with a view to making the first James Bond film. There was a great deal of argument about how the plot for it should be shaped. Fleming again wanted to make the Soviet Union the villains, while others argued that the Mafia would serve the purpose better. *Thunderball* was published in 1961. McClory had obtained an advance copy of the book and then claimed that Fleming had used a plot for a film of this work without making due acknowledgements. He filed a suit against Fleming for alleged plagiarism and against Bryce for breach of contract. McClory had a strong case, though the pros and cons of the whole affair remain highly complex. Bryce decided to settle out of court with McClory. By this means Fleming retained his rights to *Thunderball* as long as the message 'based on a screen treatment by Kevin McClory, Jack Whittingham and Ian Fleming was added to the title-page of all future editions. McClory in return was awarded the film rights to the novel, as well as the copyright to all existing related scripts and treatments. Bryce was also to pay an undisclosed sum of money to McClory and Whittingham (a writer hired to complete the screenplay) in damages as well as to pay the court costs. It was an unhappy episode in the last years of Fleming's life.

Some indication of the duration and complexity of this lengthy case can be judged from the fact that an enormous amount of documentation was involved. Brief to counsel amounted to four hundred pages: there were nearly one thousand letters, more than a hundred categories of documents and twelve scripts and story outlines.[1]

In the last few years of his life Fleming fought a constant battle against rapidly failing health. He fought it with good humour and courage, but it must have been agonizing in many ways. Right up to the very last he tried his hardest to keep up his chief recreation, golf, and to attempt occasional mildly adventurous forays around the world. Sometimes, when he was feeling quite ill, he would stay at an hotel near Brighton where he kept rigidly to himself, even refusing to see his wife.

Though Fleming had set himself up in an office in Fleet Street in 1959, he continued to attend Tuesday morning conferences at *The Sunday Times* for a while, even after it was taken over by Lord Thomson of Fleet. He showed a keen, if somewhat sardonic interest in the filming of his books and especially in actors and actresses chosen to play in the various Bond epics. Once, probably with tongue in cheek, he suggested that his friend Noël Coward should play the part of Dr No. Coward replied: 'My dear Ian, the answer to Dr No is – No, No, No.' Maybe it was with much the same sense of black humour that at a time when he had gone to a nature clinic to try to cut down his smoking he began *Thunderball* with Bond's boss reading to James a doctor's report on his health: 'This officer remains basically physically sound . . . but despite many warnings he admits to smoking sixty cigarettes a day. . . . I recommend that he should take it easy for two to three weeks on a more abstemious regime.'

Fleming, questioned by the *Daily Express* as to the state of his health when he was in the London Clinic after his heart attack in 1961, said: 'I've had telegrams from people who almost assume I'm in the morgue. But I can assure them the corpse is not completely frozen.'[3]

A source of irritation between Ian and Anne was her constant criticism of his favourite car, the Thunderbird, to which she seems to have taken an instant dislike. Though she herself never hesitated over extravagant purchases she favoured, she insisted that the car was far too expensive and fit only for younger people. Possibly one of the reasons for her attitude was that not only did Fleming take an enthusiastic interest in cars but that he had a schoolboyish passion for any new gadgets that went with them, many of which he passed on to Bond. Some of the special sabotage gadgets featured in the Bond films owe something to Fleming's own suggestions. Antony Terry records that when occasionally he drove Ian and Anne around Germany 'he was a most agreeable companion and so was she, though she used to tease and possibly irritate him by saying that my VW Beetle was more comfortable and less draughty than his beloved Thunderbird'.[4]

Fleming had very positive views on driving and drivers as well as types of cars. He was a careful driver, though he enjoyed high speed on what he liked to call 'appropriate occasions'. He often claimed that he judged people's characters on how they drove, as a result of which he made some curious judgements. 'Never trust a car driver who wears a hat,' he used to tell his friend and colleague

Philip Brownrigg. His fondness for rather special cars was reflected in his books. The early novels feature Bond driving one of the last of the 4-litre Bentleys with a supercharger built by Amherst Villiers. In the later stories this was followed by a Mark II Continental Bentley. Probably the gadgets in the Bond cars aroused as much interest as the cars themselves, and in the films made of Fleming's books these gadgets have been given even greater prominence. The whole history of what is now known as 'the most famous car in the world', the James Bond Aston Martin DB5, has been told in a handsomely produced book by Dave Worrall, sponsored by the James Bond Fan Club.[5]

This passion for cars went much further than the Bond stories, as *Chitty-Chitty-Bang-Bang* demonstrates. One wonders if this book aimed 'for ages eight upwards' had originally been concocted for the benefit of Caspar, but there is no evidence to confirm it. As Fleming wrote the book in hospital in 1961, following a heart attack, it would seem that it had no direct connection with his son. Originally published in three volumes, *Chitty-Chitty-Bang-Bang* has been modelled, filmed, and translated into twelve languages as well as being admirably illustrated by the artist John Burningham. *Teacher's World* praised the book, saying that 'the standard of writing and background details lifts them [i.e. the three volumes] above many similar books'.[6] It was dedicated 'to the memory of the original *Chitty-Chitty-Bang-Bang*, built in 1920 by Count Zborowski on his estate near Canterbury'. A year later the car won the 100 m.p.h. Short Handicap at Brooklands at 101 miles an hour. Adrian Conan Doyle, son of the creator of Sherlock Holmes, wrote to Fleming's publishers saying that the original car was given this name 'as a skit on the idea that her tremendous engine with its low revs fired once every two lamp posts', adding that the car 'could never be started with a team of less than eleven men!'[7]

Not surprisingly it was Bond's cars and the gadgets that went with them which particularly appealed to those who made films from Fleming's books. It is reported that a great deal of the budget for the film *Thunderball* was expended on gadgetry and that no less than £85,000 was spent on equipping the forty-five frogmen required for the spectacular underwater battle at the climax of the film. Of course often the gadgetry reached the realm of fantasy. There was one scene in which Bond, in his car, was being pursued by gunmen and, as they came closer, suddenly from beneath the rear bumper water was sprayed out at very high pressure, thus forcing the gunmen out of action. John Brosnan makes this comment on the film: 'We can accept most of that without too much strain on our credulity, except for the last scene. To be capable of squirting out that much water at such high pressure, Bond's car would need to contain a storage tank of vast proportions. When we remember all the other infernal devices that it's supposed to contain – machine-gun ejector seat, etc., it's surprising that there is still room for the engine.'[8]

One cannot help wondering whether, with tongue in cheek again, Fleming was trying to copy Conan Doyle by doing to Bond what the latter did to Sherlock Holmes, when he wrote *From Russia, With Love*, or if perhaps he sensed that his own days were numbered. In his obituary of Bond, 'M' referred to James having had a Scots father and a Swiss mother who were both killed in a climbing accident when Bond was eleven. David Chipp, now head of Reuters News Agency and formerly that agency's correspondent in Peking, wrote to Fleming inquiring whether he had 'done a Holmes' and deploring the killing off of Bond. Back came the following reply:

How faithless my readers are. Surely they should assume that if J. Bond must one day die, it will not be as a result of a kick on the shin. However, for your confidential information and to set your mind at rest, the following bulletin was recently placed on the canteen notice board of the HQ of the Secret Service near Regent's Park: 'After a period of anxiety the condition of No. 007 shows definite improvement. It has been confirmed that 007 was suffering from severe Fugu poisoning (a particularly virulent member of the curare group obtained from the sex glands of Japanese Glove fish). This diagnosis, for which the Research Department of the School of Tropical Medicine was responsible, has determined a course of treatment which is proving successful. No further bulletin will be issued. (signed) Sir James Molony, Department of Neurology, St. Mary's Hospital, London W2.'

In view of the above I think we can take it that JB will in due course be reporting fit for duty.

He wound up his letter by commenting that 'some of my happiest years were spent in Reuters'.[9]

A character, if used continuously by any author, as doubtless Conan Doyle, Simenon and Agatha Christie would have agreed, tends to become, if not the author himself, at least a close friend, or even an offspring. Thus Fleming made Bond's father 'Andrew Bond of Glencoe' (similar to his father?), and his mother was given the name of Monique Delacroix, which was similar to his own mother's maiden name. He also took a keen interest in devising a coat of arms for Bond, writing to his publishers in 1962 that he had been in touch with the College of Arms about the matter, saying 'Rouge Dragon doesn't think there will be any objection to using it since the line is extinct.'[10]

Meanwhile marriage was still creating problems for Fleming. So much so that during the early 1960s he wrote to his wife this undated letter from the Hotel Pierre, New York:

> This is also *my* last effort. I love you and I prove it by the efforts I make to make you happy. These efforts are not enough. All I get is a further string of complaints. When I want to do the things I enjoy, as this sudden trip to Jamaica, that is also a cause for complaint. You have had to get another man for a dinner party. . . . And now these cruel letters and cables hurled at me. Can you wonder that I'm fed up to the teeth? But for my love for you and Caspar I would welcome the freedom which you threaten me with. . . . Either we survive or we don't. There is no one else in my life. There is a whole cohort in yours. I am lonely, jealous and ill. Leave me my pleasures as I leave you yours. Above all have compassion.[11]

There is nothing Bondish about this letter: it is a plea from the heart and at the same time it seems honest as well as tolerant, as the penultimate sentence makes clear. One is left with the impression that here was a man who wanted love but found it hard to achieve; a man who liked to have a large degree of independence and was prepared to repay anyone who would grant him this.

Some might argue that two such propositions were totally contradictory, but to most modern couples the combination of devotion to one person and a sense of independence for both is probably the nearest one can get to an ideal relationship. Or, to quote Ian Fleming, 'romance is two people liking each other, but still keeping their own ways of life. Marriage can too often result in two people trying to adapt to one another and ending up hating each other'.[12]

Yet his marriage with Anne continued despite its ups and downs. 'Ian was the great love of my sister's life,' wrote Laura, Duchess of Marlborough. 'Ian had impeccable manners and great charm, but inside he was an immensely complicated character. Like my sister, he had a destructive side to him and in the later days of their marriage it seemed to me that they were determined to destroy each other. For example, my sister was always very scornful about his famous hero, James Bond.'[13]

The Duchess of Marlborough also took the view that Caspar was the one link which kept Ian and Anne together. Yet even on this subject there were differences of opinion, Fleming being far from convinced that his wife's ideas for bringing up a son were justified. He may well have been right, especially in the case of Caspar, of whom the Duchess of Marlborough wrote: '. . .he was alert, lively and full of mischief, indeed often wicked in his own special, intelligent way. He was very sceptical of the world we live in'.[14]

Fleming was convinced that fame had brought him more critics and even enemies than he had ever known before. That he realized this, at least for anyone who knew him personally, is made clear in *You Only Live Twice*. When James Bond reports to 'M' on board a nuclear submarine, fresh from his own 'funeral' at sea, 'M' says: 'Now that you're dead perhaps some of your old friends will leave you alone.' There is no doubt that occasionally Fleming made Bond answer his critics on his behalf.

In those declining years his friends backed him up to a remarkable degree, and the best of them were those who had been employed by him. In the summer of 1964, when he was quite ill, his mother died. Both his wife and his doctor told him that he was not fit to attend the funeral, but he insisted on doing so. It was a tribute to the mother who had so splendidly filled the role of a father for him.

That same year he spent August at the Guildford Hotel at Sandwich, relatively happy in the knowledge that he had been nominated as the next captain of the Royal St George's Golf Club. He had played golf there for about thirty years and, more especially since he became ill, golf had become one of his delights. He had even put the Royal St George's (renamed St Mark's) into *Goldfinger* when Bond plays a game with Auric Goldfinger: 'Bond strolled across the 500 yards of shaven seaside turf that led to the first tee. Goldfinger was practising on the putting green. . . . Bond knew that the St Mark's practice green bore no resemblance in speed or texture to the greens on the course.'

Here he continued to play golf until his death. It was after a meeting at the golf-course on 11 August 1964 that he became ill and was taken to hospital in Canterbury. There he died the following day. Noël Coward wrote in his diary: 'Now Ian has died and it is a horrid but expected sadness. He went on smoking and drinking in spite of all warnings. Annie has been distraught for months. . . . I am horribly distressed for her and miserable for myself. He has been a good and charming friend to me ever since I have known him.'[15]

One of the tragedies of the timing of Fleming's death was that it coincided with Caspar's birthday and on that very night there was to have been a birthday party at which Fleming, or so he had told friends, had intended to 'set out the facts of life' for his son. He was twelve years old on the very day his father died. Many people say that Caspar never fully recovered from the shock of his father's death. Like his father, Caspar was educated at Eton and afterwards he went to New College, Oxford, where he read oriental studies. However, after two years he left without completing his degree course. Then in October 1975 he died after taking a massive dose of barbiturates. At his inquest it was stated that he had attempted to commit suicide a year previously in Jamaica. Dr William Knapmann, deputy director of a London clinic for the treatment of psychiatric disorders, said: 'I think he felt very strongly that he had not got a proper place in life.'[16]

Anne Fleming died in July 1981. In a tribute to her Professor

Raymond Carr, Warden of St Antony's College, Oxford, wrote that 'though with a Proustian sensitivity to the nuances of English social life, her tastes were catholic. Her circle of political friendships extended from Right to Left of the political spectrum. Though somewhat of a High Tory herself, she was a close friend of Roy Jenkins, Hugh Gaitskell and Tony Crosland . . . she was an intimate friend of and correspondent with Evelyn Waugh, Francis Bacon, Lucian Freud and Sir Frederick Ashton'.[17]

The three Flemings, Ian, Anne and Caspar, are buried together close to their home at Warneford Place, Sevenhampton, and the nearby Church of St James. Ian's brothers survived him until the next decade, Peter dying suddenly while out shooting in 1971 and Richard lived until 1977.

In his will Ian Fleming provided amply for his family, and he also remembered a few of his friends. 'He generously left me and two or three other friends some money to be spent within a year on some "extravagance",' commented William Plomer. 'I would rather he had survived me. No extravagance by us can disguise though it may commemorate his absence. Whatever the money is spent on I shall think of him looking over my shoulder, curious to see how it is being used, a little ironic and (I hope) pleased.'[18]

The legacy of Ian Fleming is be found in a variety of fields. The James Bond phenomenon is still being carried on not only with new books but with old books reissued in many languages and, above all, in the cinema. To this extent the quotation from Philip Ziegler included at the beginning of this chapter is fully justified. 'The cinema industry that has grown up around Fleming's novels has been a crucial factor in keeping alive Bond's memory,' adds Ziegler, 'and yet the immense capital that has been ventured in creating these films would never have been available if shrewd investors had not realised the dramatic power of the original material.'[19]

Despite this Fleming and his reputation have actually suffered as a result of the films. Many of them vulgarized the original text as well as overdoing the display of gadgetry. In the screen version of *Diamonds Are Forever*, for example, the most vividly exciting incident was marred by the addition of a totally unnecessary and senseless murder. As Ziegler aptly puts it: 'Most of those who denounce Fleming's sadistic violence have in mind the crimes that the cinema has perpetrated in his name.'[20]

In 1989 an interesting attempt was made to portray Fleming rather than Bond at long last. As noted earlier, Charles Dance was given the role of Fleming in a television film entitled *Goldeneye*. This was shot on location in Jamaica and the United Kingdom. It was followed by *The Secret Life of Ian Fleming*, a rather more ambitious project from the American Turner Broadcasting System and starring Jason Connery, Sean's son, in the title role. This film aimed at covering Fleming's life up to the time he left Naval Intelligence, a fascinating subject but one in which many of the stories are still wrapped in mystery.

Yet perhaps the strangest legacy of Fleming is 'the strange affair of the James Bond novel Ian Fleming "wrote" six years after his death', to quote the level-headed, down-to-earth Peter Fleming, his brother. This remarkable story was written by Peter Fleming in the very year he died, 1971.[21] 'One day in October 1970, I received a short typewritten letter from an address in Hertfordshire. "I have", wrote Mr A, "some very unusual and I believe pleasurable news concerning your late brother Ian which I should like to discuss with you . . . it is of the utmost importance that you are consulted, as the personal feelings of you and your family must, I consider, be respected."'[22]

Peter Fleming felt that the reference to respecting family feelings was 'faintly ominous', but he sent a 'somewhat frigid postcard' asking the writer to ring him up. Eventually a meeting was arranged. 'Mr A turned out to be a retired bank officer aged seventy-three, gentle, sincere, with a rather ascetic appearance but a cheerful manner. He handed me a neat but bulky typescript on the cover of which was written *Take Over: a James Bond thriller* and gave me an account of its provenance.'

The background to this extraordinary story was that Mr A's wife had died three years previously and that one day in 1969 his daughter had received what was apparently an extrasensory communication from her mother, first of all giving somewhat imprecise accounts of life after death and then going on to dictate 'prepared statements' from a number of authors who were her fellow-spirits. These authors included Sir Arthur Conan Doyle, H.G. Wells, Edgar Wallace, Somerset Maugham and Ian Fleming.

Peter Fleming's summing up of what was said to be his brother's work was that it was 'particularly untrue to life' and that many of the words and phrases used were untypical of Ian. He posed some questions to be put to his brother. One of these was to inquire what were Ian's house colours at Eton. The answer came back as follows: 'Blue and yellow. No, blue and red.' The correct answer should have been cerise and grey. The Bond story from beyond contained such Bond characters as 'M' and Miss Moneypenny and it had, said Peter, 'the sort of preposterous, cosmic story-line (involving a poisonous gas which will enable its users to dominate the world) which might have occurred to Ian'. As to what he made of the whole affair, he positively ruled out chicanery by Mr A or his daughter whom he regarded as 'persons of complete integrity'. Nevertheless there was the fact that 'in eight months – between May 1970, and February 1971 – some form of intelligence caused Vera to write down, in her mother's handwriting, over 100,000 words of fiction and a great deal of subsidiary matter and to reproduce with remarkable verisimilitude the signature of one of the authors involved. . . . However you look at it, a lot of *energy* was at work here.'

However one may view this extraordinary story, The *Sunday Times* was sufficiently interested to pay £100 for Peter Fleming's article on the subject which was prominently displayed across a whole page in the *Weekly Review* section.

A strange, unresolved legacy this may have been, but one cannot altogether ignore it. Rather more positive and fully reflecting the maintenance of the James Bond cult was a report from Chicago in December 1991, which told of an American postman named Douglas Redenius who had amassed more than four thousand 'Bond items', ranging from the miniature submarine in *For Your Eyes Only*, the spear-gun from *The Spy Who Loved Me* and spacesuits from *Moonraker* to a working copy of Bond's favoured Walther PPK automatic and endless 007 products from shaving-cream to beer and photographs. Redenius's fascination with Bond started, he said, when he saw *Goldfinger* at the age of eight. His most spectacular acquisition of Bond items, he claims, is the miniature submarine which he believes will be worth £100,000 when he has fully restored it. 'It sat for several years on a dock in New York and deteriorated badly. A friend and I got it for less than £2,000. My neighbours think it's great fun that I have a submarine on my lawn. . . . Several years ago I made a bid for the special Aston Martin which was used in the early Bond films. God, I would really have loved that car. But although I put in a bid for 25,000 dollars, it eventually sold for a quarter of a million – way out of my league.'[23]

The fact is that Bond, like Sherlock Holmes and Poirot, still goes marching on. Ian would have been amused by this, but he would at the same time have loved to be able to debunk some of it.

# 12

# *The James Bond Phenomenon*

My books are straight pillow fantasies of the bang-bang, kiss-kiss variety.[1]

N ot since Conan Doyle created the character of Sherlock Holmes has there been a literary prodigy quite to compare to the James Bond phenomenon. Just as Holmes lived on in films long after Conan Doyle's death, so too did Bond after Fleming's death, not only in films but in books about Bond written by other authors, and James Bond fan clubs sprang up all around the world with a membership exceeding that of the Sherlock Holmes Society. It was almost as though a new industry had been created.

This industry began to take off during the last few years of Fleming's life. Referring to the spymania of the 1960s in the United States, the authors of *The Espionage Establishment* described how 'in the movies and on television the secret agent threatens the supremacy of the cowboy. Cereal box tops offer spy kits for children and James Bond spy toys crowd Pooh Bear on the store shelves'.[2] It could be said that to a large extent, if not entirely, Ian Fleming started the cult and that the sudden increase in spy-fiction writers dated from the late 1950s. Unquestionably it was Fleming who created the trend of what has been somewhat clumsily called the factional spy novel: it was the realism of the background to *Casino Royale* which introduced this, giving the instant impression that here was an author who knew what he was talking about, whether it was the jargon of the Secret Service, the memoranda of SIS chiefs, mixing drinks or gambling at the casino. Suddenly not only did spy fiction become the ambition of many young writers, but the feeling that it must be authentic encouraged quite a few people who had worked in various branches of Intelligence to try their luck at this new genre, of which David Cornwell (alias John Le Carré) was an outstanding example.

Some of the critics as well as the new spy-fiction writers were envious of Fleming and made this abundantly clear in all they wrote. *Time* magazine declared that 'with the help of an estimated 1,250,000 British readers, Bond has boosted Creator Ian Fleming high on the bestseller lists and into the gunsights of outraged critics. They blast him as a kind of Mickey Spillane in gentleman's clothing, his books as a cunning mixture of sex, sadism and money snobbery' and 'a bad symptom of the present state of civilization in this country'.[3] However, *Time* went on to say: 'Fleming is no Spillane. His closest U.S. opposite number, Raymond Chandler, calls him "masterly". And Elizabeth Bowen says: "Here's magnificent writing".'

Fleming frequently played down his writing and made no claim to enter the lists of posterity. Indeed on most occasions, both in print and in private conversation, he joked about his books. The epigraph to this chapter was, as noted, contained in a letter to Chandler, in which he stated: 'Probably the fault with my books is that I don't take them seriously enough and meekly accept having my head ragged off about them in the family circle. You after all write "novels of suspense" – if not sociological studies – whereas my books are straight pillow fantasies of the bang-bang, kiss-kiss variety.'[4]

Such self-deprecation, however, in no way lessened some of the attacks of the critics. Bernard Bergonzi called Fleming's attitude towards sex that of 'a dirty-minded schoolboy',[5] while Paul Johnson, at that time a critic writing in the *New Statesman*, suggested that Fleming fans were psychological cousins of prison torturers in Algeria. Le Carré seemed to hate Bond when he dubbed him 'the ultimate prostitute', but he made some amends for such comments when he rejected the suggestion that his own book, *Call for the Dead*, was an anti-Bond novel: 'That was nonsense. I'm not nearly clever enough to have done that at the time, and I wrote about the things that I knew of, the tensions in Berlin which I had witnessed . . . and I imported from my experience of the Foreign Service.'[6]

Kingsley Amis, who produced *The James Bond Dossier* in 1965, said 'it's inaccurate . . . to describe James Bond as a *spy*. Vivienne Michel, narrator of *The Spy Who Loved Me*, gave Bond a wrong label out of desire for euphony and simplicity. . . . *The Medium-Grade Civil Servant Who Loved Me* would have been more accurate as well as more acceptable. Mr Bond's claims to be considered a *counter-spy*, one who operates against the agents of unfriendly Powers, are rather more substantial'. Much later, in a short article in *The Daily Telegraph* entitled 'Would the Real 007 Please Step Forward?', Amis commented that 'Bond is not just a cipher with a gun and a slight case of priapism. Most critics have forgotten, or never taken in, his fits of tenderness, remorse and disappointed idealism, as at the end of *Casino Royale*, the first and best of the novels.' Here Amis confirms the opinions of Dennis Wheatley, Roald Dahl and many others that this first of the Bond books is the best.

Not unnaturally, the main attacks on Fleming and Bondery came from left-wing critics who were not only jealous of Fleming's success but who winced at the detailed descriptions of what they regarded as the crude snobberies of Bond's (and, as they implied, Fleming's) tastes – the vintage champagne, the Morland cigarettes with the triple gold band, the Floris bath essence and the Guerlain bath cubes. What the critics overlooked was that Britain was only just coming out of the long years of food rationing, shortages of all kinds of desirable commodities and that, subconsciously, many people yearned to be introduced to the things they had either missed, or luxuries they had never even heard of. This sense of luxury is what appealed to Fleming's readership and, shrewd psychologist that he was, those were the people for whom he catered.

Fleming, quietly rather than seriously exasperated by some of the blatantly envious criticism, once made a reply in the *Manchester Guardian*, which summed up his response to the allegations that there was 'too much sex' in his books. 'Perhaps Bond's blatant heterosexuality is a subconscious protest against the current fashion for sexual confusion. . . . I had to fit out Bond with some theatrical props. . . . I myself abhor Wine and Foodmanship. My own favourite food is scrambled eggs.' To his harsher critics he said: '. . . they have so many chips on their shoulders they should go into the timber business. I do however apologize for once making Bond order asparagus with *béarnaise* instead of *mousseline* sauce. A writer should acknowledge his shortcomings'.[7]

Two years before Fleming's death Charles Stainsby, the editor of *Today*, wrote: 'Ian Fleming's books are all part and parcel of the strange decadance which affects many of the Top People in Britain today. . . . Once upon a time this magazine ran stories by Ian Fleming. For one very sufficient reason we find Ian Fleming's work the nastiest and most sadistic writing of our day.'[8] This harsh attack was linked to the publication of *The Spy Who Loved Me*, and Fleming recorded in a letter that he was 'depressed with the reception of this book'. He went on to say that he had 'become increasingly surprised to find that my thrillers, which were de-signed for an adult audience, were being read in the schools and that young people were making a hero out of James Bond, when to my mind . . . I do not regard James Bond as a heroic figure, but only as an efficient professional in his job. So it crossed my mind to put the record straight in the minds particularly of younger readers'.[9]

One could hardly call this a cynical indifference to criticism. Nor was Fleming lacking in the ability to criticize himself and to ponder deeply on where he might go wrong in his writing. This is most marked in a letter he wrote to Michael Howard at Jonathan Cape: 'The point about Bond is that he makes a fool of himself and falls headlong into a trap. This is a change from making him the cardboard hero and I cannot help thinking it is a healthy change. There is so much danger of these books being all alike and my main satisfaction (such as it is) with the book is that a formula which was getting stale has been broken.'[10] Later in the same letter he commented: 'One simply can't go on writing the bang-bang, kiss-kiss type of book. However hard one works at it, you automatically become staler and staler and very quickly the staleness shows through to the reader and then all indeed is lost.'

The James Bond stories are much more easily absorbed and appreciated in their written form than on the screen. Very few of Fleming's original stories survived film treatment. Richard Mal-baum, one of the principal American screenwriters for the films,

says: 'While the books are great, however, they do present immense problems for the writer bringing them to the screen. "You
write too well," I told him. In *Goldfinger* the film had only four
lines from the original book.'

Nevertheless it was the film industry that set the James Bond
phenomenon on course and that led to the setting up of the
various James Bond 007 fan clubs. The principal one of these is
undoubtedly the British one, which was formed in 1979 and has
developed into a highly efficient organization. Based at Addle-
stone in Surrey, it produces a quarterly magazine, *Double-O-
Seven*, which is professionally and attractively designed and
produced. 'The club has a diverse membership in forty countries,'
says its president, Graham Rye, 'including 007 fans in the United
States, Iceland, Jamaica, Finland, Sweden, Nigeria, Brazil,
France, Japan as well as the British Isles.' In 1991 the club
absorbed the American fan club, originally started by Richard R.
Schenkman, of New York, as a result of which its membership
rose above the three thousand mark.[11]

Other James Bond fan clubs exist in Australia, Hong Kong,
Spain and Canada, but they are mainly run by enthusiastic
amateurs who produce photostat publications that feature re-
cycled news and articles from other publications. In the Spanish
resort of Costa Dorada, Eddie Royle, alias Michael Melia of the
*EastEnders* programme on television, runs the Bond Beach Club.
Meanwhile even the tourist industry has paid heed to the Bond
legend. The Dover Museum lists various places in the vicinity of
the Cinque Ports which have associations with Fleming, and some
visitors to Britain can be observed carrying *The Ian Fleming
Thriller Map*, which lists more than a hundred sites named in the
Bond books, ranging from Montreal in Canada to Miami in Flor-
ida, from Dieppe and Geneva to Leningrad and Moscow and from
Reculver Sands to St Margaret's Bay.[12]

Armed with this map, one could in the Kent countryside alone
enjoy some fascinating sightseeing, especially in that area of the
country featured in *Moonraker* and *Goldfinger*. In *Moonraker* the
Swingate near Dover is renamed the World Without Want and is
the scene of a murder. Fleming also referred to the 'Swingate
Radar Station rising like petrified Roman Candles'.

Fleming wrote his first novel in eight weeks and thereafter he consistently produced one book a year, writing between four and five thousand words a day during a similar eight-week period. The pressure on him was twofold: first to sustain the character of Bond and to pave the way to films; secondly the need for money. This last need was increased not only by the high spending of his wife and some of her extravagant tastes but by his desire to provide for his son. It was, however, far from easy to get Bond on to the screen. In 1954 Fleming made a deal with CBS television in America to broadcast a one-hour adaptation of *Casino Royale*, with Barry Nelson as an American James Bond and Peter Lorre as the villain Le Chiffre. He did not see the programme himself, but Clare Blanshard, his former secretary who was working in the Kemsley Newspapers office in New York at the time, wrote a highly critical review of the film and sent it to Fleming. He was more amused than upset by her comments. After that there were various approaches by film-makers, but little came of them. Ian Hunter of the Rank Organization bought the film rights to *Moonraker* but did nothing about it. Then Fleming was asked by Henry Morgenthau of NBC to work on a proposed series provisionally called 'Commander Jamaica'. This project never came to fruition. Then followed the complicated affair of Xanadu Productions.

In these latter years the fact that Fleming was in the bestseller lists created certain tax problems. It was partly to help him cope with these that he bought up a defunct company, Glidrose Productions. Then in March 1964 he was advised for tax reasons to sell 51 per cent of Glidrose Productions. He knew that his health was deteriorating; by selling more than half of the shares in his business to a public company, Glidrose would be treated as a separate entity upon the author's death. He eventually negotiated the sale with his golfing friend Sir Jock Campbell (now Lord Campbell of Eskan), Chairman of Booker Brothers, McConnell & Company Ltd, and for £100,000 Booker Brothers became co-owners of James Bond. This was also done with a view to securing the maximum benefit for his wife and his son. Since then Glidrose Productions Ltd and, since 1972 as Glidrose Publications Ltd under the direction of Peter Janson Smith, has sustained the James Bond genre with outstanding success.

Ill-health, the prolonged strain of the case brought by McClory and the knowledge that it was Bond who mattered most (that James and James alone was the key to his future) undoubtedly affected the writing of Fleming in the last few years of his life. There is every indication that latterly he found writing more of a chore than a pleasure and that at times he became bored with it all. Even then he tried to make a joke of the whole business. On St Valentine's Day, 1955, he wrote to Ivar Bryce as follows:

> Hi! Biscus,
> Have written 70,000 of a new Bonderie but now with only two chapters to go I am in a bad fix as the heroine suddenly got a crush on a divine Lesbian hood who commands a women's gang yclept The Cement Mixers. Miss Pussy Galore, for that is the lizzies Moniker, has got my heroine parting her hair three ways in front of the mirror and I don't see how Bond can possibly get between them with only two chapters to go.[13]

The critics were of course ready to pounce on any signs of deterioration in the Bond stories, but Fleming still had stout defenders in Kingsley Amis and William Plomer. Amis in his obituary of Fleming said: 'One cannot forget *Moonraker* for the vivid, rounded depiction of its villain, Hugo Drax, and what is probably the most gripping game of cards in the whole of literature.'[14] Plomer summarized Fleming's books as 'brilliant, romantic fairy-tales in which a dragon-slaying maiden-rescuing hero wins battle after battle against devilish forces of destruction, and yet is indestructible himself: an ancient kind of myth skilfully re-created in a modern idiom. They are, like life, sexy and violent, but I have never thought them corrupting. Compared with some of the nasty stuff that gets into print, they have a sort of boyish innocence.'[15]

Kingsley Amis was the first person to carry on the Bond tradition with *The James Bond Dossier*. It is an amusing analysis of the adventures of Fleming's larger-than-life hero and helped to counteract the reaction against the Bond phenomenon by many critics, including even some of Fleming's former self-proclaimed admirers. Yet it is true that Fleming tended to make Bond less credible in his later books, too much of a figure for the screen rather than the printed word. And a new school of writers emerged who loathed Bond, seeing him as a neo-fascist and a 1950s version of Bulldog Drummond.

Yet despite this reaction the demand for Bond stories and films remained unsatiated. At the time of Fleming's death some 20 million copies of his books had been sold and fifteen of his works had been filmed. The books had been translated into eighteen languages, including Catalan and Turkish; and they were being read in Iceland, Thailand, Japan and Brazil as well as all over Europe and North America. As recently as 1985 George Grella, a distinguished and respected critic of spy and detective fiction, wrote of Fleming:

> Whatever his present standing among readers and critics, Ian Fleming accomplished an extraordinary amount in the history of the thriller. Almost singlehandedly he revived popular interest in the spy novel, spawning legions of imitations, parodies and critical and fictional reactions, thus indirectly creating an audience for a number of novelists who followed him in the form. Through the immense success of the filmed versions of his books, his character James Bond became the best known fictional personality of his time and Fleming the most famous writer of thrillers since Sir Arthur Conan Doyle.[16]

John Gardner was one of the spy-fiction writers of the early 1960s who originally detested the character of James Bond. He had spent five years in holy orders, including a spell as an RAF chaplain, before realizing he was fundamentally an agnostic and turned to writing. It was Gardner who created the anti-hero of Boysie Oakes as almost an antidote to Bond. But eventually he tired of Boysie Oakes, despite the fact that *The Liquidator* was an instant success. Even more surprising, he signed a contract to write a series of updated James Bond adventures, the very books he had set out to debunk in *The Liquidator*. His first Bond book was *Licence Renewed* (1981), in which he made his version of Bond rather more akin to the screen portrayal of the character than that of Fleming himself. It must have been a tremendous task for Gardner to follow in the Fleming track, a hard enough job for anyone, and also to carry on with the quite different type of spy novel he had initiated. Ten more Bond novels written by Gardner have been published: *For Special Services* (1982); *Icebreaker* (1983); *Role of Honour* (1984); *Nobody Lives Forever* (1986); *No Deals, Mr Bond* (1987); *Scorpius* (1988); *Win, Lose or Die* (1989); *Brokenclaw* (1990); *The Man from Barbarosa* (1991) and *Death Is Forever* (1992).

Gardner wrote to me from his home in Charlottesville, Virginia, about the problems of what he called 'upgrading Bond':

> After ten years of it (with my own books nicely squeezed in between) I have at last persuaded Glidrose to let me write a more realistic Bond. It will be out later in the year – *The Man from Barbarosa*, but the U.S. publishers are being difficult. If you tackle Bond from a real viewpoint and make him behave, use tradecraft etc., he does fade into second place, but I think it works, so, thank heavens, does Glidrose.[17]

Probably few other spy-fiction writers have been taken so seriously by a potential enemy as was Fleming by the powers-that-be in the old Soviet Union – by both the KGB and the GRU, the military espionage organization of the USSR. The Russians' interest in what they could learn from spy-fiction writers was first aroused by Somerset Maugham's *Ashenden*. The GRU discovered the facts about Maugham's undercover work in Russia during the First World War and urged that a study should be made of all British spy books in the Soviet Union henceforth. But it was the advent of the James Bond stories that caused the Russians to take this task much more seriously. Partly because they knew of Fleming's role in Naval Intelligence, partly through knowledge of his Mercury foreign service, the Soviet hierarchy believed that he was still in Intelligence and that the Bond books were a form of Cold War propaganda. What disturbed them even more was that the Bond stories were being translated into so many languages.

The results of this trend of thinking in Moscow were quite astonishing. Until the 1950s espionage had been a dirty word in the Soviet vocabulary: it was something in which only the decadent Western world indulged, whether in reality or in fiction. Suddenly it was realized that to compete with the kind of thing Fleming was doing, it was necessary to publish competitive spy fiction; in other words, to beat Bond at his own game. The Soviet hierarchy, thinking that to exploit such tactics from the Soviet Union would be somewhat blatant, arranged that Bulgaria should be used as the country in which to counter-attack Fleming. The Bulgarian novelist who responded to the KGB's request in this matter was Andrei Gulyashki. The object of the operation was to popularize secret agents of the Soviet Union as noble heroes who protected the fatherland and at the same time to improve the image of both the KGB and GRU at home just as much as overseas. The man behind the operation was Vladimir Semi-chastny, the newly appointed head of the KGB in 1961, when he contributed an article to *Izvestia* on this very subject. Gulyashki then invented an ace Soviet spy named Avakum Zakhov, whose main mission in life seemed to be to destroy James Bond, 'this supreme example of imperialistic espionage', as he was dubbed in Moscow.

There was some slight apprehension in London at first by Flem-ing's publishers that this was the beginning of a piracy of the James Bond name. It was partly owing to this that support was sought from Kingsley Amis to help maintain the Bond legend. He did so in his novel *Colonel Sun*, written under the pseudonym of Robert Markham, published in 1968. Gulyashki's book, *Zakhov Mission* (1966), was an instant success and was serialized in *Kom-somolskaya Pravda* (the Soviet youth paper) under the title of *Avakhum Zakhov versus 07*. The Bulgarians were unable to get copyright permission to use Bond's name or '007', so they got round it by deleting one zero from the code-name. The book was translated into English and published in the United Kingdom in 1968. Zakhov, needless to say, was a much more proletarian figure than Bond, not least in his culinary tastes, which seemed to concentrate on cabbage and noodles!

For a while afterwards the USSR launched a series of stories of their own favourite secret agents. In February 1966 Vadim Kozhevnikov's novel *Sword and Shield* was first published in the literary monthly *Znamya*, and it was generally assumed that Colonel Rudolf Abel provided the prototype for Kozhevnikov's hero, Alexander Bolov, whose surname was a transposition of Abel in Russian. Shortly before his death in Moscow in 1971 the redoubtable Colonel Abel, who had proved such a superb spy and spymaster combined while in the United States, introduced a film called *The Dead Season*, a spy thriller about germ warfare experiments in the Western world.

Since then spy fiction has taken off in the USSR. In the 1980s it was as popular in the Soviet empire as in the West. Julian Semyonov, one of Russia's chief spy-fiction writers, is today one of the richest men in the Soviet Commonwealth, with a large apartment in Moscow and two other homes, including a villa on the Black Sea. Before Markus Wolf, the former East German spymaster who planted thousands of agents in NATO countries, was arrested, he gave an interview. Asked who he thought were the best spies, he replied: 'Maybe the English were the best, these James Bonds, because they were the ones I knew the least about.'[18] This was twenty-seven years after Fleming's death.

What, it may be asked, prompted this special interest in Fleming's work apart from the fact that the Russians knew that he had served in the NID and hazarded a guess that he might be using journalism for carrying on a certain amount of Intelligence work? The answer, according to KGB files released since the creation of the new Russian Commonwealth, is that as a result of reading *Casino Royale* they were looking out for examples of factual background which Fleming employed in his novels. One KGB document refers directly to Fleming's mention of SMERSH in that book and asks for a regular check on 'any similar references to our organization or personnel which the author may make in one form or another'. SMERSH was a contraction of *Smyert Shpionam* (Death to Spies), an organization that was started by the *Cheka* as *Osobyi Otdely* and existed in the Second World War when it was given the job of tracking down German agents in areas previously occupied by the Nazis. Ivan Serov was deputy chief of SMERSH in this period. It was dissolved in 1946. Presumably the Russians were concerned that Fleming might have learned that SMERSH had been incorporated in the OKR (*Otdely Kontrrazvedki*), a counter-espionage service after 1946. Fleming referred to

SMERSH again in *From Russia, With Love*, describing it as 'the official murder organization of the Soviet government'.

It was Nikolav Khokhlov, who defected from the USSR in 1954, who provided invaluable inside information which Fleming used in *From Russia, With Love*. Khokhlov had been sent to Frankfurt by the KGB to arrange the murder of George Okolovich, leader of the anti-Soviet NTS organization, but instead he went to Okolovich's apartment, warned him of the plot and then defected to the Americans. In *From Russia, With Love* the head of SMERSH says 'We do not want another Khokhlov affair' while talking to the chief of the KGB. Khokhlov knew all about the latest gadgets in Soviet aids for secret agents: 'I could have had any technical assistance or gadgets I wished,' he told Lord Bethell. 'There was, for instance, a new model of a fountain pen with electric firing apparatus that was almost made for the job. It looked like a Parker.'[19]

From my own knowledge, I am aware that Fleming sought for all manner of background information from the Soviet Union the type of background that would be useful for inclusion in his novels. On one occasion he asked me to arrange for him to have full details of the Trans-Siberian Railway, which covered some 8,952 kilometres. He had already obtained some information on the subject from a railway buff in Geneva, but he asked me to obtain 'full details of what such a journey from Moscow to the Pacific would be like; of compartments and berths; food supplied and how served; how conductors control movements, tickets and even entry into those secret midnight parties they are supposed to hold; also any colourful portrayals of females to be found *en route*, even the samovar girl. . . .'[20]

Our own correspondent in Moscow at that time duly arranged for a friend to make the full Trans-Siberian trip from Moscow to the Pacific and to let me have his notes on his return. These notes were duly passed back to us through a foreign embassy's diplomatic bag. It was a trip which at that time took seven days and the train usually started off with some five or six hundred passengers, few of whom, however, went all the way.